THE COMPLETE
PROBLEM
SOLVER

"THE COMPLETE PROBLEM SOLVER provides a disciplined approach to problem solving. It will surely become a reference for both business and personal decision making."
> —Gary L. Tessitore
> Executive Vice President
> J.I. Case Company, Inc.

"I found THE COMPLETE PROBLEM SOLVER to be a practical, useful and thoroughly enjoyable book on the essence of management, which is solving problems. It is highly readable and provides good tips on how to tackle virtually every challenge a manager might face. It should be on every manager's book shelf."
> —Ronald G. Anderson
> Chairman
> General Re Financial Products Corporation

"THE COMPLETE PROBLEM SOLVER provides down to earth examples of a fail-safe, systematic problem solving process. This book does not reveal the *right* strategy—instead it instructs the reader on how to solve the problem. Arnold presents a framework simple enough for a child's use, yet so comprehensive it should be a cornerstone to broad world-order situations. It works."
> —James E. Bachman
> President and Chief Executive Officer
> The New Hampshire Insurance Company

"John Arnold has an excellent, disciplined method of quickly analyzing root causes of problems and applying systematic steps to reach the best among several possible decisions with hard and soft information which executives know exist in almost every situation. THE COMPLETE PROBLEM SOLVER is easy reading and full of good examples."
> —James L. Bast
> President and Chief Executive Officer
> A.B. Dick Company

THE COMPLETE PROBLEM SOLVER

A Total System for Competitive Decision Making

John D. Arnold

JOHN WILEY & SONS

New York • Chichester • Brisbane • Toronto • Singapore

Library of Congress Cataloging-in-Publication Data
Arnold, John D.
    The complete problem solver: a total system for competitive
  decision making / by John D. Arnold.
      p.   cm.
  Includes Index.
  ISBN 0–471–54198–2
    1. Problem solving. 2. Decision-making. I. Title.
HD30.29.A76   1992
658.4′03—dc20   91–43604

Printed and bound by Courier Companies, Inc.
10 9 8 7 6 5 4 3 2 1

CONTENTS

Contents

DEDICATION

To the many thousands of managers throughout North America, and in Europe and Latin America, who have applied *The Complete Problem Solver: A Total System for Competitive Decision Making* to their business, professional, and personal lives—and who have found that it made a real difference.

ACKNOWLEDGMENTS

I am indebted to the several hundred companies over the past 24 years that have applied the concepts and managing tools of this book to the challenging issues and opportunities confronting their organizations.

Every example in this book is an actual application by clients resolving particularly crucial issues they faced.

In a true sense, the men and women who managed these experiences, drawing on *The Complete Problem Solver* methodology as their key *integrative* mechanism, really wrote this book.

I wish to thank Keith Parsons of the ExecuTrak Systems professional staff for following up client projects to develop some of this material and Steve Bennett for helping me edit the book.

PREFACE

Every era presents unique challenges to people in business. But the 1990s offer unprecedented opportunities and dangers, especially for American companies. Here are just a few of the major issues with which executives, in large and small companies alike, and government officials must contend:

- The changing racial composition and mores of our population.
- A highly accelerated pace of product and industry obsolescence.
- The emergence of techniques that have rendered traditional American manufacturing second rate.
- American management no longer viewed as the "fountain of wisdom."
- "Japan, Inc."
- The selling of America (i.e., hundreds of this country's power elite working to advance other nations' political and economic interests over ours; the attitude, "if it's legal, it's OK," regardless of the ethics).
- A united Europe.
- The shift from ideological conflict to private–public trade and foreign aid initiatives to reduce cultural and political constraints on our ability to compete globally.
- The impact of global stock trading.
- International cross–company product–teaming and global networking.

How will we deal with these challenges? The old ways simply won't suffice—the issues are too complex and far-reaching. For example, we can't tackle problems of product obsolescence by looking for simple "screwdriver" fixes. And we can't address global competition by just turning up the heat on old marketing tips.

Instead, we need a pro-active means for examining global problems and challenges in a new light and developing solutions unique to the problems of the 1990s. Top executives must realize this need and adopt a system that will enable managers and employees *at all levels* to make the right choices. Such a *complete thought* system must provide a decision-making framework that enables business people and government officials to consider ALL relevant data—that means value judgments as well as hard facts. The system must recognize that decision making and problem solving reflect both art and science, intuition and analysis. The challenges at hand can be met only by those who can combine insight and wisdom with facts and figures.

That's what this book is all about. In the pages that follow, you'll learn a method of competitive decision making that has been refined and tested for the past 24 years in situations ranging from domestic marketing problems facing small firms and major strategic/cultural dilemmas threatening multinational corporations to infrastructure, trade policy, and foreign aid quandaries that challenge government agencies; also, from serious concerns confronting religious organizations, research institutes, and health care agencies to issues blocking the economic revitalization of entire geographic regions.

The method allows you to arrive at the best possible solution by considering every factor that should influence your decision. You can use it to solve internal organizational problems, to resolve asset and risk management concerns, to develop and transfer technology among R&D centers and manufacturing plants, to systematize information technology, and to build international product–teaming arrangements systematically aligning and focusing people, business processes, and technological resources. You can even use the method to sort out issues in your personal life and make the best possible home life and career decisions.

The global competitive clock ticks on.

Whether you are trying to develop a marketing plan that will allow your company to compete more effectively against Pacific Rim countries, make inroads into Eastern Europe, or build cross–company or intergovernmental alliances, the *Complete Thought Process* will serve as a guide. Use it regularly, and it will enable you to create, rather than merely cope with, your future.

Martha's Vineyard, Massachusetts   John Arnold
February 1992

INTRODUCTION

Think to Win

Imagine that you're the president of a company that manufactures automobile tires. After years of experimenting, your chief of research has just announced the development of a new material that could easily extend the life of a set of radials to 100,000 miles. "It's a great day for car owners," he beams. But the cheers from your R&D department are quickly drowned out by cries from the sales and marketing departments. "We're in the tire *replacement* business—this stuff could put us out of business," warns your national sales director. What should you do with the miracle material? Lock it up? Use it in all your products? Offer it only for a high premium? Offer different "blends" at a graduated price? Find some other application unrelated to tires?

Clearly, you need more data to make an informed choice. But what data do you need, and how do you know that you need it? In other words, using the tire example as a model, can you describe how you go about making decisions? If you're like most people, this is a very difficult question to answer. Few of us have been taught how to analyze situations and make decisions. Yet, somehow we all subconsciously develop our own problem-solving and decision-making methods, tailored to our personalities and shaped by our upbringing and schooling. And we use it everyday, from the moment we wake up until the moment we turn in. The dozens, even hundreds, of decisions we make each day range from the mundane—what clothes to wear or what to eat for breakfast—to the critically important—should we make this acquisition? Should we adopt this new marketing strategy? Should we make this investment of time and money? and so on.

If all of your decisions yield the desired results 100 percent of the time, you probably can close this book. Chances are, though, that your "hit rate" is less than perfect, in which case you can improve your decision-making skills by adopting the proven methodology presented in this book. It presents a decision-making framework that I have developed during my 30 years of consulting with executives and managers of some of the most successful companies in North and South America and Europe, as well as with a variety of non-profit organizations.

The framework encompasses what I call the *Complete Thought Process*, which allows you to explore and weigh three critical elements of any decision: the causal elements (Root Cause Analysis); your various choices (Option Analysis); and the upside and downside potential (Risk Analysis). Taken together, these elements provide you with a simple yet powerful means for making decisions in your business, professional, and personal life.

BENEFITING FROM THE COMPLETE THOUGHT PROCESS

Whether you're the head of a multinational corporation, a middle manager in a medium-sized company, or a lone-wolf entrepreneur about to launch an enterprise, you'll find that the process described in the following pages will help you think more clearly and do a more effective job. Once you begin using the *Complete Thought Process* as a routine way of tackling problems and making decisions, you'll find yourself:

- Homing in on the right issues to tackle first. Too often, decisions are made based on the *wrong* issues. The *Complete Thought Process* ensures that you'll focus on the core elements of any situation. You'll make the right choice because you're addressing the right issues.
- Reducing complex situations to simple components. Every problem, no matter how monumental it seems, consists of simple components. The *Complete Thought Process* helps you break down a problem into manageable chunks, then develop solutions that work for the problem as a whole.
- Solving problems and making decisions with a balance of intellect, intuition, and emotion, rather than purely from the head or the gut. By applying the steps of the *Complete Thought Process* in both your business and your personal life, you'll be able to assess the true nature of any situation, as well as the opportunities and dangers it affords.
- Making decisions based on all factors pertaining to the situation. The *Complete Thought Process* forces you to capture *all* of the relevant data.
- Making decisions that are easier to sell to other people. Even if the buck stops at your desk, you still need buy-in from the people who will actually translate your choices into reality. The *Complete Thought Process* leaves a complete thought trail—you can easily justify your position and demonstrate how you arrived at it through a balance of values and logic.

Your organization, too, will benefit as more people begin using the *Complete Thought Process*.

- Better information capture systems—the *Complete Thought Process* tells problem solvers what questions they'll need to ask and what data they'll need to obtain to resolve the issues at hand.

- An "early warning" system that reveals emerging problems and opportunities. This in turn makes it possible for people to take the fastest and most effective corrective action.
- Less "arm waving." Problem solving and decision making become a productive activity that leads to satisfying solutions.

Finally, The *Complete Thought Process* facilitates input from all parties affected by a particular problem. As people become more used to contributing to the process of solving problems, making decisions, and analyzing risks, they will by necessity develop improved communication skills. These skills will in turn translate into a more productive work environment, higher quality, and better job performance.

PUTTING THE COMPLETE THOUGHT PROCESS TO WORK FOR YOU

The *Complete Problem Solver* is organized in a fashion that lays out the three components of the *Complete Thought Process*. Chapter 1 provides an overview of the each of the three major components—Root Cause Analysis, Option Analysis, and Risk Analysis. Three parts then explore the three types of analyses in depth. The first chapter of each of the parts describes the mechanics of the particular analysis; subsequent chapters in each part show various applications of the analysis at various companies. The fourth and final part describes how the three analyses are integrated into the *Complete Thought Process*, again with illustrations from a variety of organizations. This part will test your understanding of the process by questioning you about it, then providing you with the "right" answers; giving you "management whodunits" to solve and decisions to make, with "approved solutions"; and suggesting final techniques to help you apply the *Complete Thought Process* under tight time pressure. The Epilogue suggests how organizations and the United States can apply this process to strengthen global commitments.

Ideally, you'll read the book cover to cover first, to get a sense of what the *Complete Thought Process* has to offer. (Don't worry about trying to remember each detail of each type of analysis on the first pass; the process will become automatic as you use it on a regular basis.) Then go back to Part I, Root Cause Analysis, and try to ferret out the causal elements of a pesky problem in your business. Try the analysis with new problems as they crop up each day, both at work and at home. Soon, you'll gain confidence as you experience success as a "root cause" sleuth.

Continue the same process with Option Analysis and Risk Analysis, again starting off simply and then tackling more complex problems. Over time, you'll find that the *Complete Thought Process* has become your routine way of looking at the world; what may have seemed like a long series of steps in the beginning will become an automatic sequence that you quickly apply to any situation. And the more transparent the process becomes, the more you'll enjoy the benefits of making clear and informed decisions.

Just one caveat: Don't try to use all three components of the *Complete Thought Process* "off the shelf"; though the process and the analyses are simple, more than likely they represent a departure from your normal way of sizing up the world and making a decision. If you try to jump-start the process, you may get frustrated and give up on it too early. You spent years developing your present decision-making system, and you can't replace it overnight, just as you can't wake up one day and decide that you'll run a marathon to get into shape. Go slowly, and enjoy the process of learning a new system—you'll also gain some interesting insights into your personal thought style.

THE COMPLETE THOUGHT IMPERATIVE

Every decision, no matter how trivial it seems, has an impact on your organization's operational effectiveness. That's why it's critical for each and every member of a management team (ideally, everyone in the company!) to be analyzing problems and making decisions with the *Complete Thought Process*. This is especially important in the 1990s, when competitors in Europe, the Pacific Rim, and elsewhere are forcing American companies to rethink how they do business. Yet, among the cries for more efficient manufacturing processes, higher quality, employee empowerment and consensual management, more innovation, trade restrictions, and other issues that are supposed to level the playing field, no one has focused on improving the *quality* of thought in American companies. In other words, let's rethink how we think. What better place to start than with your own—and your organization's—decision-making system?

PART I

Root
Cause
Analysis

CHAPTER ONE

Who Dunnit: Root Cause Analysis Explained

Following sweeping changes in healthcare legislation, the top management of an insurance company anticipated a flood of calls from businesses that would have to comply with the new laws. To answer questions from current policyholders and supply potential new clients with information and quotes, the company tripled the staff of its Inquiry Department. A reasonable move? Sure. But instead of staying even with the flow, the staff found itself drowning in a sea of phone calls and written requests. Several months after the backlog began accumulating, the situation reached crisis proportions with over 9,000 inquiries waiting to be processed. At that time, inquirers had to wait an average of 8 weeks for a response.

Management responded by firing the department supervisor and replacing him with someone who had considerable experience managing Inquiry departments. Despite the personnel change, there was still no improvement, and management took a closer look at the situation. One executive noted that the backlog concerned only medical questions. So she asked the $64,000 question: "If faulty organization on the part of the former supervisor had really been the cause of the problem, why weren't there backlogs in auto, disability, and other types of insurance?"

Why, indeed? "Why" is one of the most important words in the problem solver's lexicon. And as you'll see in this chapter, an understanding of why things happen is a fundamental step in solving any problem and making the right decision. Once you understand the "root cause" of a situation, you can move on to the next two steps of the *Complete Thought Process*, choosing your options and assessing the risks. But that's getting ahead of ourselves. This chapter provides you with a detailed explanation of *Root Cause Analysis*; the next chapter illustrates root cause in action. (We'll return to the mystery backlog at the insurance company a bit later in this chapter, and see how the company's management easily could have determined and resolved the origin of the problem by applying Root Cause Analysis.)

TOOLS OF THE TRADE

Root Cause Analysis begins with a recognition of a gap between what should be occurring and what (allegedly) is *not* occurring. In other words, you recognize that there is a situation of sufficient concern for which you need to find correct *cause*. Something has gone either worse than you hoped (a problem) or better than expected (an opportunity). In either case, you need to discover its true cause in order to take effective action. The conventional approach to finding cause, once you recognize a problem, is to search out all the possible explanations that might fit the known facts. Unfortunately, this is extremely inefficient and often a waste of time since you have not narrowed (or "dimensioned") the problem. Root Cause Analysis provides an identical set of tools for defining a problem or opportunity, establishing boundaries, determining what's distinctive about the situation, and then zeroing in on the probable cause.

Before delving into the Root Cause process, it's important to adopt a problem solver's mind-set. This entails developing a new sense of awareness of the problem you're trying to solve or the opportunity you wish to understand, as well as an awareness of how your own perceptions and values will affect the analysis. The latter is particularly important, since each of us makes a cognitive and emotional contribution, even during so-called objective scientific investigation. By "scanning" your internal environment, you become more aware of thoughts and feelings that may jade the analysis (Am I angry? Do I have a "hunch" that X or Y will be cause? and so on).

You can also scan the external world in which the problem or opportunity occurs, looking for what deviated from your expectations. Thinking in terms of deviations is important because it will ultimately allow you to arrive at the probable cause. Moreover, it will help you ask the right questions and collect the right data.

In addition to building the right mind-set, scanning has the benefit of providing a kind of early-warning and "opportunity detection" system. And the sooner you detect that something is going awry or is different from what you anticipated, the closer you'll be to the source of the real problem or opportunity. This is important because time is the enemy of the problem solver. Over time, data gets lost or distorted (the "*Rashomon Effect*"); the original issues get lost as the problem transforms; and feelings, opinions, and emotions infuse the problem, making it more difficult to identify the real issues at hand. Also, it is typically easier to find the cause of something that occurred 5 minutes ago than 24 hours ago. Not only is memory fleeting, but the shorter the delay in tackling the problem, the fewer the opportunities for the situation or your perceptions of it to change, let alone information to be distorted or hidden.

One final aspect of mind-set needs to be approached before explaining the Root Cause Analysis process—you need to see the world in terms of differences rather than similarities. This often is challenging, because most people have a natural tendency to look for commonalities with other problems they have experienced: "Gee, this problem is exactly like the one we had three months ago in Purchasing." This kind of association carries with it the built-in assumption that the current problem must have the same cause(s) as the one that occurred several months ago. Although this may seem like an economical way to organize and draw from your experiences, it may also lead you on a wild goose chase. There may indeed be 6 similarities with the previous problem—but there may also be 19 differences! And it may only take *one* key difference to highlight the real nature of the problem and the fact that it has a distinctive cause. So by linking a problem with others that have taken place in the past, chances are that you'll merely hide the unique cause of the current problem. As you'll see in the remainder of this chapter, looking for distinct particulars about a given issue is the key to successful causal analysis.

Now, on to the actual steps used in Root Cause Analysis ("1P/6D's" for short—Prioritize → Define → Describe → Distinguish → Diagnose → Destroy → Decide).

1. *Prioritize.* List the order in which problems or opportunities should be dealt with (i.e., based on seriousness of impact, urgency, amount of data immediately available, and whether it is within your area of authority or sphere of influence).

2. *Define the Problem or Opportunity.* Instead of asking "What's the problem?" which is totally open-ended, ask "What is not happening that *should be* happening?" or "What is happening that *should not* be happening?" By phrasing the question these two ways, you'll help eliminate built-in assumed causes. The definition should be stated on a General, Observable, and Factual (GOF) level. Doing so lessens the chance you have built in any assumed causes or limited the scope of your search. Sim-

ilarly, ask, "What is going better than I expected?" If anything is, then seek out its root cause so you can fully exploit the situation.

3. *Describe the Problem.* Every problem or opportunity has three dimensions: identity, location, and timing. *Identity* refers to who or what is involved. (Which people, which products or services, which departments, etc., are the object and nature of the concern?) *Location* describes where the problem is occurring (at East Coast headquarters, first detected at incoming vendor inspection at the sister plant, reported by four specific customers, etc.). *Timing* tells us when a problem or opportunity is happening in terms of the calendar and clock (since 5:00 P.M. on January 29, continuously or with a definite periodicity rather than in sporadic episodes, etc.). By describing these dimensions, you specify and put boundaries around a problem. This in turn makes it possible to logically test and verify possible causes of the problem.

Each of the three dimensions has a magnitude or scope (only one of the four product lines—*identity*; branch offices in Buffalo and Syracuse—*location*; from February 1 through February 5, but only from 4 P.M. to 6 P.M. and not any other time of day or night—*timing*). The more precise you can be regarding each dimension, the more you'll be able to narrow your search for the most probable cause. Conversely, the less precise your data, the less the chances you'll home in quickly on the right cause.

Another important aspect of describing the problem or opportunity is to specify what it *is not*, again using the dimensions of *identity*, *location*, and *timing*. For example, we can inquire what things *do not* display a specific defect (the *identity*), where it *is not occurring* (the *location*), and when it *is not happening* (the *timing*). The act of defining what the situation *is not* further delineates the boundary around the problem or opportunity.

For example, the fact that sporting-goods sales were off-target in your downtown Boston store in the first week of May begins to define the problem. The additional facts that sporting-goods sales were not off-target in the New York, Philadelphia, and Washington stores in the first week of May significantly tightens the boundaries of the problem. Whatever the cause, it must account for the fact that it's only sporting goods, only downtown Boston (not New York, Philadelphia, or Washington), and only part of the month of May.

Finally, describing what the problem (the "crime") is as well as what the crime is not paves the way for the next step in the analysis, looking for distinctions.

4. *Distinguish.* Once you've contrasted (or distinguished) a problem or opportunity in terms of what it is or is not, where it is happening and where it is not happening, and when it occurs and when it does not occur, it is far easier to look for what is distinctive to each dimension. (Bear in mind that the scope or magnitude of each dimension can harbor important distinctions.) If something isn't distinctive, it can't be the probable cause—how else could it account for the unique dimensions of the problem or opportunity? Logically, characteristics that distinguish the "crime is" (or opportunity) component of your problem description from the "crime is not" elements must be regarded as *bridges* to the possible causes. The fact that New England has an unusually cold spring would differentiate the Boston store from the other stores, which are situated in areas that experience a warmer spring. Although in this case the cause might be traceable to the effect of one distinction, often two or more distinctions operate together to bring about problems or opportunities.

5. *Diagnose (Develop a Hypothesis).* Based on the distinctions you uncovered in Step 4, you can draw hypotheses as to what well may be the most probable cause. Looking at each distinction, ask yourself, "In what ways could that distinction have caused the problem or opportunity in terms of the precise characteristics of the crime is/crime is not dimensions?"

6. *Destroy the Hypothesis.* The goal here is to rigorously test your ideas about the most probable cause through destructive testing. This is done by using the dimensions of the crime and what's outside of it as a blueprint against which to test each hypothesis. In other words, the cause must be able to explain why a particular event that happened did indeed occur, exactly as described, rather than another event (i.e., why *this* defect occurred and not *that* one; why you've experienced a sudden, unexpected surge of orders for a particular product and not for others, etc.). It also has to explain both sides of the description of the problem—why it occurred at only one location and not at the other specified locations, at a particular time and not another, and with the particular scope and magnitude of each dimension.

7. *Decide What to Do Next.* Once you arrive at what you believe is the true cause, you can further validate the cause or continue to analyze for additional causes, this time at lower levels; or you might determine appropriate corrective or opportunistic action. Ultimately, your judgment and experience will tell you when you have "staircased" the analysis to a level at which you can take effective correction action. Consider the sporting-goods example recently described. Although the cold New England spring may test out as the most probable cause of sales being off in the Boston stores, you could act on your determination of the probable cause. (This would

be done by discretely determining whether competing stores in the area exhibited the same symptoms with regard to the identity, location, and time dimensions.)

Although this may seem like a lot of steps to go through to find the cause of a problem, the time is well worth it. After all, if the problem or opportunity is significant, the payoff from knowing how to deal with it will be far greater than your investment of time at the Root Cause stage. This is typically far less expensive in terms of time, energy, and money than taking one stopgap action after another in a vain attempt to eliminate the unknown cause of your concern. (Just remember the last time an inexperienced auto mechanic tried to fix your car by process of elimination!) Also, be assured that the more you use the process, the more automatic and habitual it will become. Accomplished problem solvers move from Step 1 to Step 7 with minimal awareness that they are working with a structured process; Root Cause Analysis simply becomes their normal way of responding to the world about them.

ROOT CAUSE IN ACTION

Now that you've seen the bare mechanics of Root Cause Analysis, let's return to our opening example, which involved an insurance company that suffered from a major backlog in the Inquiry Department. Had Causal Analysis been performed at the time the problem was first identified, it would have become evident early on that medical insurance inquiries were the sole culprit. The job of one supervisor might have been saved, and months of customer ill will, organizational frustration, and tens of thousands of dollars in unnecessary costs could have been avoided.

To begin with, the positive problem statement (what the crime *is*) would have revealed the *description* in Table 1.1. Notice how answering descriptive questions about what the crime *is* reveals two key pieces of information:

Table 1.1 Priority "Crime": Excessive Backlog of
Medical Insurance Inquiries

Dimension	The Crime Is
What (identity—scope)	Severe backlog of medical policy inquiries regarding premium payments—up to 9,000 inquiries
Where (location—scope)	Main office at data-collection phase
When (timing—scope)	Since mid-1990 and averaging 7 weeks behind

1. Not only is the problem unique to medical insurance inquiries, it more specifically involves medical inquiries about premium payments.
2. More specifically, the backlog is occurring at the data collection phase.

Table 1.2 expands the description by specifying what the crime *is not*. The description of what is *not* involved in the

Table 1.2 Priority "Crime": Excessive Backlog of
Medical Insurance Inquiries

Dimension	The Crime Is	The Crime Is Not
What (identity—scope)	Severe backlog of medical policy inquiries regarding premium payments—up to 9,000 inquiries average	Normal backlog; other concerns (i.e., errors, incompletes, Auto, Home-owners); Life insurance inquiries or inquiries on benefits, renewals, change of status; fewer or more than 9,000 inquiries
Where (location—scope)	Main office at data-collection phase	In the field; preceding or following phases
When (timing—scope)	Since mid-1990 and averaging 7 weeks behind	Before mid-1990; normal maximum of 6 weeks or less behind; beginning after mid-1990

crime has now put much tighter boundaries around the problem and has paved the way for our efficient search for distinctions. Before we even start looking for *distinctions (contrast* and *differentiation)*, we can see that the funneling of the information during the problem description phase has pinpointed some sharply contrasting pieces of information that must contain a number of *distinctions.*

For example, there must be something unique to premium-payment inquiries that differs from inquiries about benefits, renewals, change of status, cancellations, and so forth—why else would the problem involve only medical insurance payments? Likewise, there must be some difference between the data collection phase and other processing phases, since data collection is the only *location* where the backlog is occurring. Finally, why didn't the problem exist prior to mid-1990? There must be something peculiar to the time period beginning mid-1990.

Asking the question "What differentiates each element of what the crime is from what it is *not?*" yields the information in Table 1.3. The identification of *distinctions* enables you to hypothesize logically about what may be the most probable (as opposed to theoretically possible) cause because these distinctions are based on the unique dimensions of the crime (i.e., what it is and what it isn't, where and where not, when it is occurring and when it isn't, and the scope of each). These hypotheses are the ones to test first against available information on the problem. Following are the possible causes in this actual situation.

- The department may not be large enough to handle the volume.
- Procedures aren't adequate for the volume of payment inquiries—needed data is not readily available; it takes too much searching to locate the data.
- New people may not be properly trained.
- The new supervisor did not manage properly.
- Too many policy changes may have been implemented.

Table 1.3 Distinguish

Description	Distinctions
What (identity—scope)	Largest volume
	Requires considerable investigation, information searching, and adjustment of records; inquiries don't fall into routinely handled categories
	All policy inquiries on the rise since July 1990
	Increasing number of changes in all policies since June 1990
	Payment inquiries increasing from normal 10 percent of total to 65 percent since July 1990
Where (location—scope)	Only place where these types of inquiries are handled
	Department has no records of its own from which to retrieve this data; has to use resources of another department
When (timing—scope)	New people added in April 1990; new supervisor, September 1990

Destructively testing these possible causes (that is, trying to destroy them by comparing them to what is known about the *identity*, *location*, and *time*—and scope—of each) would result in Table 1.4. The testing process shows that of the five hypotheses, only *one* uniquely fits all dimensions; that is, it cannot be destroyed on the basis of what is and what is not. Therefore, it is the most probable cause. The final step would involve verifying that the hypothesis is correct, which would be easy enough to do; simply time the process of answering several typical medical inquiries.

Once satisfied that the probable cause is the *true* cause, you would move on to correct the situation. Obviously, firing the supervisor is not the best solution. But this is what happened at the company in question, and it illustrates how too often actions are taken without testing the assumed causes against the facts and dimensions of the crime. Where something has gone

Table 1.4 Destroy

Possible Causes	Destructive Testing
Department not large enough to handle the volume	Doesn't explain why only medical inquiries are affected.
Procedures inadequate for volume of payment inquiries	Doesn't explain why holdup is only at data-collection phase.
Needed data not readily available; takes too much searching	Would explain *everything* contained in the "crime is" and "crime is not" dimensions considering the increased volume of individual inquiries
New people not properly trained	Doesn't explain why only these unique inquiries.
New supervisor not managing properly	Doesn't explain why only these unique inquiries.
Too many policy changes	Doesn't explain why only medical inquiry payments are in question.

wrong, effective corrective action can only be taken after thorough analysis of the problem to remove its Root Cause. Moreover, it's essential to deal with the problem at the Root Cause level to help both correct it and *prevent* it from recurring.

Also, as you can see from this analysis, in-depth probing often is required to uncover just what it is about each *distinction* that could have caused the problem. There is always some kind of change distinctive to the crime (or a unique combination of changes) that precisely fits the facts (i.e., is unique to the problem) especially the time dimension, since anything distinctive or unique to the time of a problem, in contrast to the situation before the problem occurred, is by definition a Change. The only exception to this rule is when what *should* have happened and what *actually* happened have never been the same. (In other words, there has *always* been a deviation between the expectation and reality!)

To understand the subtle importance of change, consider a manufacturer that unveiled a new line of sweaters. The company backed the introduction with an extensive magazine advertising campaign and point-of-purchase displays. Curiously, although the new line was making a hit in most areas of the country, sales were below expectations in one city. An application of Root Cause Analysis enabled the sales manager to pinpoint the cause. Table 1.5 shows the complete reconstruction of the crime.

At first blush, everything pointed to the sales rep who set up the displays and assisted in counter sales as the area of cause. (The problem couldn't have been the promotion itself—it was working well elsewhere.) But what was this man doing that resulted in the sales decline? It couldn't have been that he

Table 1.5   Priority "Crime": Low sales

Describe	*The Crime Is*	*The Crime Is Not*
What (identity—scope)	New sweater line sales off, decline 80% off-target	Normal complaints Slight decline Other new lines Other sweaters
Where (location—scope)	Greater Albany area, Stores A & D	Other cities, Stores B & C in Greater Albany area
When (time—scope)	Past 2 weeks	Before

	Distinctions
What (identity—scope)	Special promotion, point-of-purchase displays
Where (location—scope)	New sales rep set up displays and assisted with counter sales for a day
When (time—scope)	New sweater line launched

turned customers away when he was there, because sales were good that day—they dropped from the next day on.

After much diligent questioning, the sales manager found out that the sales rep was assisting in counter sales to the point where he was actually ringing up sales on the cash register. Each sale that he rang up was one that a store employee *didn't* ring up. For every such sale, that employee lost a commission. This irked the employees to the extent that they began pushing competitive brands of sweaters—hence, the decline in sales!

Before analyzing this problem, the sales manager was considering four courses of action:

1. Give the department managers in those stores some "push" money (an incentive-building reward for each sweater sold).
2. Give the salesclerks "push" money.
3. Increase the advertising in that city.
4. Put on a special price promotion in that city.

Although such actions might have increased the quantity of sweaters sold, they would have automatically reduced profit from these sales. Worse, they would not have treated the cause of the problem or prevented its recurrence. Once the sales manager knew the Root Cause of the problem, he was able to work out a much less expensive arrangement; the clerks simply received the commission for sales made by the company sales rep.

ANALYZING WHY THINGS GO RIGHT

So far in this chapter, we've used a logical system of analysis for determining the cause when things go wrong. Now let's look at a situation that is not frequently analyzed for cause—when things go especially well. Looking back at our case of the new sweater sales campaign, suppose that sales in Albany had surged ahead of any other city. There are several reasons that a sales manager might want to know the cause, the most obvious being that if a success formula can be figured out, that could be applied to other locations. Also, identifying the factors responsible for the Albany "boom" would allow the manager to better assess the costs of achieving the spectacular sales level; perhaps the costs dramatically diminish the profitability of the product, which of course would be counterproductive. Finally, identifying the cause of the success might enable the sales manager to devise less costly alternatives for obtaining the same results elsewhere.

The concepts used to determine why things go right, of course, are identical to those used to find out why things go wrong. The sole difference is that the distinctions isolated in The Crime *Is* column on the table show what went right!

Too much management time is invested in looking at what's wrong with a company, a product, an employee, and so forth. The real payoff lies in being pro-active, by scanning what is going *especially well*, then analyzing for the Root Cause of the positive deviation. You then have a better chance of sustaining the benefits and translating them to other products, customers, locations, and so forth.

SUMMARY

The Root Cause Analysis process is in no way intended to be a substitute for intelligent thinking. Rather, it is meant to be a tool for focusing your experience, technical knowledge, intuition, and judgment in the pursuit of identifying and testing *distinctions* that reveal the true underlying cause. When you come right down to it, the process is "applied" common sense—simple, logical, and practical!

But if that's the case, then why don't people naturally apply it? Because they haven't analyzed situations in this way, or they don't follow a logical sequence. The latter is critical and requires discipline; you can't shortcut the process by jumping down from Step 1 to Step 6 in the hopes of getting to the cause more quickly. Patience might be a general virtue; for the problem solver, armed with the 1P and 6D's (Prioritize → Define → Describe → Distinguish → Diagnose → Destroy → Decide) it is an essential quality.

CHAPTER TWO

Jack and the Magic Black Box: Root Cause Analysis in Action

Like everyone else at Display Technology Inc. (DTI), engineering manager Jack Carter was proud of his company's contract with the Department of Defense to build a major subassembly for a new radar system. The subassembly, known as the "multi-frequency graphic processor" (MFGP), consisted of a microprocessor located on a printed-wire "motherboard" as well as numerous ancillary boards that contained special function chips and circuits. Unfortunately, about a year into full production, DTI's motherboards began failing quality control tests at an alarming rate, causing costly remake and jeopardizing the company's ability to deliver on time. How can Carter and his team go about pinpointing the problem and saving DTI's multimillion dollar contract?

DTI's problem might, at first glance, seem purely technological and far removed from the concerns of most managers and executives. But this very "screwdriver" aspect makes it an excellent tool for illustrating Root Cause Analysis; after all, you probably won't have any preconceived notions or opinions about why the motherboards are failing. In the next section of this chapter, we'll eavesdrop on a meeting in which Jack leads his people through a Root Cause Analysis session. Note how he gently moves people along while soliciting information. You can do the same when using Root Cause to solve *any* kind of problem.

The second section of this chapter brings technology a bit closer to home. You'll work through an example in which a husband and wife must solve a problem with two television sets. Again, the subject matter is somewhat removed from the concerns of general management, so you can approach it as objectively as possible. But it's also within the realm of most people's experience, and you should easily be able to identify with each step. Now let's tune into the crisis at Display Technology Inc.

WHAT'S BUGGING MOM?

Before beginning the session, Jack holds up a card listing the steps in the 1P/6D's analysis, just to refresh everyone's memory about the process:

> Prioritize → Define → Describe → Distinguish → Diagnose → Destroy → Decide

Prioritize/Define/Describe

Since the problem involved only the motherboard, there is nothing to prioritize, and Jack moves straight to the problem definition: "OK, folks. Let's reconstruct the 'crime' here— we'll nail this thing down in terms of identity, location, and timing. Remember, we're looking for what the crime *is* and what it *is not* [identity]; where it is occurring compared to where it is *not* occurring [location]; and when it is happening and when it is *not* happening [time]. Let's also see if we can pin down the scope or magnitude of each dimension—that can be very helpful in determining the ultimate cause."

Caren Matthews responds immediately: "The problems are only happening with the motherboard units, and not the other boards. Our tests have shown that the failures are caused by an open circuit in the soldered section of the motherboard—definitely not the assembled parts. An average of three motherboards per week are failing QC tests, and of these, the problem is confined to 100 of the 10,000 circuits."

"Any other unique identifiers?" asks Jack. He waits a few moments, then moves on. "How about the location—where exactly is it occurring?"

"It only happens in the Display Production area—not in any other DTI shop," answers Bob Weston.

"Does that wrap it up for location?" Jack asks. Everyone in the group nods, so he concludes the "dimensioning" of the problem by asking about the timing.

"It started just after February 10, 1990," reports Joel Baker.

"Just after? Does that mean the 11th, or some specific time on the 10th?" asks Jack.

"From the data I have," Joel responds, "it looks like it started sometime that weekend."

"Okay, it would help pinpoint cause better if we knew precisely when this 'crime' was first detected. But since we don't, could you make a note to try to get that information? In the meantime, let's move on. So far, we've defined the boundaries to some extent. Let's review them before moving on to the next phase of the analysis." Jack takes the large sheet of paper upon which he has been writing down the group's answers and tapes it on the wall. (See Table 2.1.—You might want to review it yourself before moving on.)

Table 2.1 Priority "Crime": Motherboards failing

	Crime Is	*Crime Is Not*
What (identity)	Restricted to the motherboards	Ancillary boards
	Soldering on the motherboard	Assembled parts
	One to three motherboards per week failing QC tests (scope)	All (or more than three) motherboards
	About 100 circuits (magnitude)	Other 9,900 circuits
Where (location)	DTI's display production area	Other divisions or shops
When (time)	On or shortly after February 10, 1990	Prior to February 10, 1990

Distinguish

Once the team has defined the dimensions of the problem, Jack starts asking for *distinctions*—what differentiates the problem; that is, what is unique about it? This will provide the most direct path to the probable cause of the problem.

Again, Caren Matthews is the first to respond: "You know, Jack, one distinction I see looking at the *time* dimension is that there *was* a change from 'FSED' [full-scale engineering development] to production on in late January."

"Good point!" confirms Jim Clark. "We weren't the only ones who went from development to production in that same time dimension; I verified that the printed wire board [PWB] vendor also made the shift, at that same time. That's also distinctive."

Jack nods and then writes both comments on his chart paper. He then motions for any other distinctions from his staff members.

"One distinction I see, Jack," says Martin Kettler, "lies in the *location* dimension—we use a different soldering process from our sister divisions."

Jack notes the distinction and then asks, "Are there any

other distinctions we can draw out by contrasting what the crime is with what the problem is not; where the crime happens in contrast with where it doesn't; and when the crime occurs in contrast with when it doesn't?"

From the back of the room, Glenn Peters replies: "Well, the vias [tubular conductors that pass through the layers of the printed wire board] are located in the same 100 circuits that show failures. That is a uniqueness compared to the rest of the circuits that *don't* show failures."

"Excellent!" says Jack. "Any others?" Jack takes advantage of the following silence to offer one of his own: "I notice that the motherboard is twice as large as any other board."

"That's correct," says Dave Wilcox. "The MFGP motherboard is also larger than any other printed wire board we've ever built. That's also peculiar to the situation."

Pam Simpson, seated next to Jack, adds her own observation; "You know, the motherboard is a 'rigid flex assembly' [which refers to a type of material that partially bends]—the only one in the whole MFGP unit. That's certainly distinctive."

When the team seems to have exhausted the distinctions, Jack holds up his chart and says, "All right, let's review our list and see what we have here."

Distinguishing Factors
1. Changed from FSED to production, late January.
2. Motherboard vendor changed from prototype shop to full production shop in late January.
3. Soldering process was different for this shop in contrast with other DTI divisions.
4. Vias located only in 100 circuits that show failures.
5. Motherboard twice as large as other motherboards.
6. Motherboard larger than any other PWB previously built.
7. Motherboard is rigid flex assembly.

Diagnose

The next step is to develop a diagnosis, a set of hypotheses based on distinctions. "Any thoughts on what may be our culprit?" Jack asks the group.

"I'd like to offer something based on the *time* dimension," says Dave. "Maybe the printed wire board vendor changed the manufacturing process for the motherboard."

"Okay, that's a good one," confirms Jack. "Anybody else?" Pam quickly offers the following: "Well, looking at the third distinction we have up there, maybe the production soldering process is the problem."

Taking off on what Pam had just suggested, Glenn adds his own hypothesis. "I think the vias may be causing the problems—perhaps there's poor soldering inside the vias themselves."

"Good, very good." Jack compliments the group as he writes down their ideas. "Another hypothesis?"

"Maybe the motherboard is just larger than we can manage—perhaps it's just heating up in some areas and causing the circuits there to expand and short out. That could be the problem—oops, I mean cause," offers Caren.

"Okay, and any others?"

"Well," says Glenn, "Could be that the rigid flex assembly is causing the problem—it's different from anything else in the unit."

When no one else offers any hypotheses, Jack holds up the chart. He also glances at his watch and congratulates everyone on coming up with the suggested causes, each one drawn from a distinctive feature of the crime, in *less than 10 minutes*. The chart recaps the following hypotheses:

Diagnoses (hypotheses about probable cause)

1. PWB vendor may have changed motherboard manufacturing process.
2. Production soldering process.

3. Poor soldering in vias.
4. Motherboard size.
5. Rigid flex assembly.

Destroy

"Now, let's put these to the test," says Jack. "We'll use destructive testing to try and shoot down the hypotheses—then we can arrive at the true cause. As I read off a hypothesis, call out if you can make it unravel. OK, we'll start with the first one: The PWB vendor may have changed his motherboard manufacturing process when he went into full production."

"That's an easy one to verify," says Caren. "Just pick up the phone and ask. But right now we can't shoot it down; we don't have enough information."

"How about the second one, the production soldering process?" asks Jack.

Glenn quickly responds. "Well, I think that's pretty doubtful since other boards in the MFGP unit use the same soldering process as the motherboard and they're fine. So it can't be the soldering."

Nods from around the room show agreement with Glenn's assessment of the second hypothesis.

"And the third one, maybe poor soldering in the vias?"

Dave responds, "We'll have to check into that one further, Jack, so we can't shoot that one down either, based on our description and the limited amount of data we have."

"How about the fourth one, the size of the motherboard?"

"That's questionable since the temperature profile data shows that there are no differences over the entire board area," answers Pam.

"Number five?"

"That's a no-brainer," exclaims Bob. "Other DTI shops use the same rigid flex assembly and haven't reported any problems."

Table 2.2 Destroy

Diagnose (Hypotheses)	Destructive Testing
1. PWB vendor may have changed process	1. Not enough information to shoot down
2. Production soldering process	2. Doubtful cause—other DTI shops use same solder process
3. Poor soldering in vias	3. Not enough information to shoot down
4. Motherboard size	4. Doubtful—tests show uniform data over board surface
5. Rigid flex assembly	5. Shot down!—other divisions use same rigid flex assembly

Jack writes down Bob's remark, then holds up the results of the destructive testing. (See Table 2.2.) After everyone has a chance to view the chart, Jack sums up the analysis, saying, "It looks like we have reduced the possibilities to just two candidates here: The vendor may have changed his manufacturing process, unbeknownst to us, or poor soldering at the vias. Let's further test those and work with them."

Jack then suggests a break, during which team members can investigate the two possible causes. When the group reconvenes, Dave announces that the vendor process for building the motherboard was continually changing from the start of the development phase (early in 1988) to the present, yet, there were no failures prior to February 10, 1990. Also, the open circuit always occurs at a vias on failed samples.

"How do you know that the vendor didn't introduce a problematic change shortly before February 10?" asks Jack.

"Easy," Dave answers. "The change in production occurred three months before, and we had no problems with boards manufactured during that period."

"That leaves the soldering in the vias as the only probable cause!" Jack says triumphantly.

Cheers of victory ring out from across the room. "Now

let's verify if this is actually the cause, and if so, take corrective action."

Decide

Further bench testing quickly verified that the soldering in the vias was the root cause, and simple refinement to the production techniques eliminated the problem. Within a week, DTI was once again churning out defect-free motherboards and MFGP units that met government standards. The project had been saved, and each member of the team had learned a new technique that would forever change the way he or she approached problems.

Now let's bring the Root Cause Analysis technique a bit closer to home, and see how a weary couple dealt with a pesky problem right in their living room.

AS THE DIMMER TURNS

The following account (as told to the author after a consulting session) illustrates how Root Cause Analysis can easily be applied to mundane—but irritating—problems that inevitably crop up in your personal life.

Linda and George Robinson had just returned from a three-week vacation and flopped down in their recently remodeled living room. George flipped on the television set so they could catch up on the news in "civilization." While they waited for their favorite newscast to start, they looked around at the fine job that the decorators had done in the living room while they were gone. Well, almost perfect—to their annoyance, they discovered a pattern of horizontal lines rolling up the TV screen. No matter what dials George turned, the lines kept appearing, like lemmings marching to the sea.

"Darn decorators," George cussed as he threw up his arms in frustration. "They messed up the television—I knew we shouldn't have left them here alone while we went on vacation!"

Linda, the cool head of the couple, put her hand on George's shoulder. "No problem—we'll just go into the family room and watch the news in there. We'll deal with the living room TV tomorrow." But to her surprise, the TV in the family room displayed the same racing stripes!

George fumed, then grabbed the phone and began to dial the decorator's number. Linda suggested that Carl's office wasn't likely to be open at 6 P.M. on Saturday. Besides, why not try out the Root Cause Analysis method she had learned at her company? She gave George a capsule summary of each step of the "1P/6D's" process and by the "Decide" phase, George had calmed down and said, "Oh, why not—what do we have to lose?" Here's what happened.

Linda picked up a pad and a pen and said, "Our first step is to prioritize the problem. In this case, we only have one problem, so that's it! So there's not much to prioritize!"

"That was easy enough," said George.

"Just wait." The next step is to begin with a problem definition—what's not happening that should be happening? Think of yourself as a detective. We're going to reconstruct the 'crime.' "

George abruptly answered, "The crime is obvious: The blasted decorators broke our TVs and they shouldn't have."

"Do we know that for a fact, George?"

"Well, no."

"Right. So let's just stick to what we know to be factual—what we observe."

"OK, Linda. Both TVs are busted!"

"Good, that will be our working definition of the crime. Let's try to describe the crime in terms of its *identity*—what's happening; its *location*—where it's happening; and the *time*—when it's happening. At the same time, let's also describe the problem in terms of what's *not* happening, *where* it's not happening, and *when* it's not happening.

"Hey Linda, why bother with what's not happening?"

"I asked the same question in the session at work, George, and found out that this should help us put boundaries around the description—that will make it easier to pull out *distinctions* later on. The distinctions will tell what is unique about the problem and lead us to the most probable cause."

"Oh really?" queried George.

"Trust me," Linda answered with assurance.

The two then wrote down their observations about the identity of the crime. "Now," said Linda, "there are two lines, about three inches apart, making their way up the screen. So it's not more than two lines, or more or less than three inches apart. Right?"

"Right."

"OK, let's move on. The TV sets are definitely affected. But how about appliances, like our radio?"

After further inspection, they found out that no other appliances were affected.

"OK, getting back to the lines, they're continuous, thin, and rolling horizontally. They are *not* vertical or dashed. And it's not a matter of a blank picture screen or a solid black screen either."

"All this is pretty obvious, dear. It's probably the darn cable company!"

"When we went through this at the plant, George, we tried to hold back from jumping to the causes we suspected all along. We worked on describing the information, rather than guessing at what the causes might be. If we had guessed wrong and didn't realize it, we'd be working on a problem that didn't exist! So we postponed guessing about the crime and its cause until we had uncovered the *relevant* facts. So just bear with me for a few minutes, will you?"

"OK, OK," George snorted.

"Now, the picture is messed up, but the sound is still clear. The problem is on all channels and not just one channel. It's also on both our cable channels and the regular broadcast channels. Whatever the channel, the lines roll from the bottom to the top, rather than top to bottom. Right?"

"Yeah," George said, finally showing some interest. "We really do know a lot about the situation. Maybe it wasn't Carl or the cable company. But that's speculating."

"You got it. Let's continue with the *location* dimension."

"Simple—the TV in the living room and in the family room."

"Well, don't we have another TV upstairs?"

"Yep."

"Let's check it out."

"Oh, that one isn't going to work either—why bother?"

"You're jumping to conclusions again, dear. Let's check it out."

George ran upstairs and then hollered, "You won't believe this—this one works fine!"

"Ah hah!" Linda said as she jotted down this finding. "So it's the TV in the living room and the TV in the family room, but it's not the TV in the bedroom!"

"Well, let's get even more specific," said George, feeling shown up. "It's the TVs on the west wall and in the center of the house, not on the north, south, or east walls or in the corners."

"Very good," Linda responded. "You're getting the hang of this. Now we'll wrap up this phase of the analysis by noting the *time* of the crime. Let's see, it happened as soon as the TV was turned on, right? It wasn't delayed, was it?"

"Nope, the lines appeared as soon as we turned on the sets."

"And they were working fine before we left on the trip?"

"Correct. The sets worked fine on November 25—I watched a football game. But here we come back on December 16, and they're not working."

"Let's take a look at what we've learned," Linda said as she tore off several sheets of paper from her writing tablet and passed them to George. The dimension summary contained the information in Table 2.3.

After the two had reviewed the dimensions of the problem, Linda suggested that they move on to identifying the key distinctions of the crime. "George, can you think of any sharp contrasts or differences between what is and is not happening?"

"One big difference I see between what's wrong and what is not wrong lies in the *time* dimension when the decorators were here."

"OK, that's a valid distinction. But what other distinctions can we pull out of our description?"

Table 2.3 Priority "Crime": TV's don't work properly

	Crime Is		Crime Is Not
What (identity)	Two downstairs TVs (living room and family room) Only video All channels Both cable and broadcast Two lines, 3" apart Small, rolling, continuous lines Roll from bottom up	What (identity)	Upstairs TV, radio, other appliances Audio Just one channel Either cable or broadcast One or more than 2 lines; more or less than 3 inches apart Large or solid vertical or noncontinuous lines. Blank picture or full solid picture Roll from top down
Where (location)	Two TVs—one in living room, one in family room on west wall, center	Where (location)	TV in the bedroom South, north, or east walls Corners or sides of west wall
When (time)	December 16, 6:00 P.M. As soon as TV turned on	When (time)	When last observed—November 25, 6:00 P.M. Delayed

"Hmm. Well, it's pretty strange that the problem happens with the two downstairs TVs and not the TV in the bedroom. By the way, the two downstairs TVs are the same brands."

"That could be distinctive—we'll put that down; what else?"

"Uh, based on the *identity* when we described the problem, and looking at the description now, it seems like it's got to be electrical—like it's coming through the wires, the airwaves, or something."

"That could be distinctive, but let's mark it as an 'inference' because we don't know it's a fact. Here's what we have so far in the distinguishing features department:

Distinguish

Decorators in house

TV brands the same

Electrical interference (inference)

"Now we can move on to the next step—diagnosing the situation by developing hypotheses based on the unique elements of the crime. Go to it, George—start hypothesizing."

"The first one involves the decorators' being here. So one hypothesis is that they dropped the TVs, maybe dumped paint into the air vents—something like that."

"We'll jot it down. How about the next one—electrical interference?"

"The only electrical fixture the decorators had anything to do with was the new lamp in the living room; maybe it has something to do with that."

"Fine," Linda says with a giggle. "How about the third— the difference in the TV brands? What's the hypothesis we can form out of the distinction that the two downstairs TVs are the same brand? Oh, wait a second! What brand is the one upstairs? Is it the same?"

"I don't remember—guess I'd better go take another look." George left and returned quickly. "It's the same brand, but a different model from our two TVs here."

"OK, then it's not the brand but the model that's distinctive. So I'll strike out *brand* and write in *model*. Now, what's a logical hypothesis?"

"Maybe this model just falls apart."

"Sounds like too much of a coincidence, but that's getting ahead of ourselves—I'll put it down. Anything else."

"Hey, here's something we haven't talked about: It could be a cross in the wiring."

"George, the only thing wired was the dimmer switch and you did that. What about something in from the airwaves, like Paul's ham radio next door?"

"That's a good hypothesis."

"Thanks! So far these look like some possibilities. Some look better than others, but before we judge them, are there any others?"

"Nope—none that I can think of."

"Great. Let's work then with this list."

Diagnose (Hypotheses)
Decorators may have dropped the TVs
New lamp in the living room
TV models
Cross-wiring may have occurred on dimmer switch
Ham radio interference

"Now we need to destructively test each hypothesis. Let's see which ones we can immediately knock down. Your kind of action, George! Let's take the first one—the decorators dropped or damaged the TV sets on the first floor."

"Not too likely that they'd be damaged so severely—there are no signs of dents, marks, or scratches. Also, why would they move the set in the family room? They were only working in the living room."

Linda jots down George's thinking, then asks about the next on the list—the new lamp in the living room—again giggling.

"Hmm, I don't see how the addition of a new lamp could have any effect."

At that point, Linda bursts out laughing. "George, the lamp isn't new—my mother gave it to us as an anniversary present last September, and it's never interfered with the TV sets! You *do* remember, don't you?"

"Oh yeah, sure," George says.

"Now then," Linda continues, satisfied that she's made George dance on the coals a bit. "How about the third hypothesis, that the problem is related to the fact that the two sets are the same model?"

"Shouldn't make any difference. Besides, the set in the living room is used ten times as much as the set in the family room—if anything, the one in the living room should go on the fritz long before the family room set. So I'd nix that one."

"Good," says Linda, jotting down his answer. "Onto the cross-wiring."

"We really can't shoot that one down—not until we get some more data."

"Okay, and the last one?"

"No way—if we had ham radio interference, it would affect the set upstairs as well."

"Well, that seems to leave us with only one possible culprit, the dimmer. According to the 1P/6D process, we need to get some additional information to prove that that's the probable cause. Now what about the dimmer—didn't you install that just before we left?"

"Hmm, you're right. And if it's the dimmer, it wouldn't affect the upstairs television set. For sure, the upstairs TV is not affected."

"How about the next hypothesis, George: the wiring of the dimmer? After all, didn't you put a new dimmer switch on that light?"

"Oh yeah—if I cross-wired it with the outlet in the living room and family room, maybe we'd get some kind of interfer-

Table 2.4   Destroy

Destroy (Hypotheses)	Facts	"Shootdown"
Decorators may have dropped the TVs	No dents, scratches.	**X**
New lamp in the living room	Not new—false assumption!	**X**
Cross-wiring may have occurred on dimmer switch	Need more information.	**?**
TV models	Models identical—but one used 10 times more than the other.	**X**
Ham radio	Why isn't TV upstairs affected?	**X**

ence on the TV set. And the fact that we don't have the problem upstairs would support that idea. Now, Carl's people only put in a new fixture, but hey, you know, now that I think of it, the funny thing is, the light has always been on when we've tried to watch the TV."

"This sounds like we're really getting close, George. But let's stick with the method, and list our options for destructive testing." Linda shows George the chart on Table 2.4.

"Looks like there's only one hypothesis that needs further checking out—the dimmer," grumbles George as he reviews the chart. "And that's an easy one to test; all we have to do is . . ." George walks over to the dimmer switch and turns off the light. Miraculously, the lines vanish from the screen. (Actually, there's nothing miraculous about the situation at all—George had inadvertently cross-wired the outlet and the lamp, creating what is known in the electrical engineering business as "60 cycle hum.") "Well, I'll be," George whistles to himself as he walks back to the couch. "The case is solved! But I still think somehow Carl's people fiddled with the switch!"

"Oh come on, George," Linda says with a laugh as she gently elbows her husband's rib cage. "I hope you've learned something from this experience—don't jump to conclusions.

It's so much more practical to follow a systematic method for solving problems and making decisions than using 'seat-of-the-pants hunches.'"

(Total time for the analysis? 15 minutes—just in time for the couple to catch the weather portion of the news.)

* * *

In both cases, the problem solving worked because people weren't allowed to jump to conclusions. They learned to focus their energy on the process, even when their minds were racing ahead.

Practice using the Root Cause Analysis method in your business and personal life. Write out your own characterizations and scope of the identity, location, and time dimensions of "crimes" you're trying to solve, or the cause—unknown opportunities you've detected (i.e., things going better than you expected) that you'd like to exploit. Once the data is in chart form, your experience will help you see the situation in a new light; seemingly small elements may take on monumental significance. Each chart also serves as a cornerstone in your reconstruction of the crime. And by listing the data in chart form, you'll force yourself to *precisely* answer questions regarding what's going wrong or especially right, where it's occurring and where it is not occurring, and when it is and is not taking place. Eventually, thinking in terms of the "1P/6D's" and organizing your thinking in chart form, whether in your mind or on paper, can become your everyday method of dealing with life's problems and opportunities—to your advantage!

PART II

Option Analysis

CHAPTER THREE

Anatomy of a Decision

In 1990, the rock group Milli Vanilli became an overnight sensation with chart-busting hits such as "Baby Don't Forget My Number," "Take It As It Comes," and "More Than You'll Ever Know." Actually, "group" is something of a misnomer—the band primarily consisted of two perfect, macho-looking singers who turned out to be just that—too perfect. Shortly after receiving a coveted Grammy Award, it was revealed that they were only lip-syncing their songs while other people did the actual singing, and the would-be superstars returned the award in disgrace.

If only they had "smoked out" the issues when they first decided to lip-sync, they undoubtedly would have avoided the serious consequences they suffered when their charade became a scandal in the music world. And when nominated for the award, they again had the opportunity to "come clean" and explain the situation. Instead, they just "took it as it came." Deciding to act rather than waiting for the hammer to fall might have caused ill will or a retraction of the nomination, and certainly the award. But it certainly would have saved them a great deal more grief down the line.

* * *

Rock stars aren't the only ones who sometimes fail to assess their situations before making decisions that have serious consequences; business people—even the best and the brightest—also find themselves in difficult, even dire, straits because they made a decision without really understanding the scope of the situation and the consequences. For instance:

- Look at American banks—if they had more carefully thought out their decisions to make real estate investments and loans to Third World countries, they would not be in the plight they're in today.
- Ford, GM, and Chrysler also demonstrated poor judgment when they joked about the VW bug and early Japanese models as being toys. Their decision to ignore a potential threat from overseas has cost them dearly in recent years. To paraphrase Milli Vanilli, they simply "took it as it came," and found themselves competing with "more than they could ever know."
- Seven out of ten acquisitions fail to meet the acquirer's financial objectives. Nearly two of every three are outright failures. The reason? Most parent companies fail to adequately assess the full situation before making an acquisition decision and wind up with incompatible or unruly children.

Before looking at a battle-proven decision method (Option Analysis), let's step back for a moment and ponder a question that is rarely asked: When you make a strategic decision, what really happens? For most people, the answers will be:

1. You invest your valuable time and effort (and possibly that of others as well).
2. You commit some type of material resources (money, time, space, equipment, people, etc.).
3. You may well affect how others will feel not only about the situation but about you, negatively or positively—in some way, your own self-image and reputation can be strengthened or damaged.

4. You either open or close future options for your life and well-being—and that of business associates, family, and others.

But who really thinks about these issues when making a decision? For most people, decision making is a matter of personal style. How many people do you know who might be described as the following?

Ostrich: Head in the sand, avoids decisions.

Rambo: Ready, Fire, Aim! Shoots from the hip first, asks questions later. Trigger finger bypasses brain. Decisions usually cause destruction and "dead bodies."

Chicken Little: All decisions are crisis decisions and must be made on the basis of what is known now, without further research and thought.

Univac: Reduces all decisions to a "numbers game"—no human element, feelings, or subjectivity allowed.

Bleeding Heart: Makes decisions purely on an emotional basis.

Janus: Makes decisions, but too insecure to stick by them.

The Pro and Con Artist: Also known as the "waffler." This person sits on the fence. Balances pros and cons and ends up with zero—and a great deal of anxiety.

And what's *your* style? Whatever it is, you can benefit from looking at a well-proven method that forces you to fully understand what it is you're trying to decide, explore what you're hoping to get out of the decision, and choose the best options.

The idea of using an explicit decision-making system is nothing new; during the past 25 years, several decision-making techniques have been developed. Although these techniques have helped people to better focus on what they're trying to achieve, by and large they have failed to produce a generation of better decision makers. In general, they're either too abstract to be useful or so purely quantitative or mechanistic as to ignore the emotional component that underlies every decision.

In the following pages, you'll learn about a method that is both rigorous and "humanistic"; that is, it considers basic personal and business values, emotions, and feelings to be important, while at the same time providing you with an orderly means for quantitatively evaluating means for achieving your goals. This method, referred to in this book as *Option Analysis*, forms the second leg of the *Complete Thought*. It entails the following seven steps:

1. Smoke out the issues.
2. State your purpose.
3. Set criteria.
4. Set priorities.
5. Identify options.
6. Test your options against your criteria.
7. Troubleshoot and refine your choice.

Now let's examine each step in detail, so you can begin putting the method to work for you. Even though it may take a while to become "fluent" in using the method, you'll experience immediate benefits just by becoming aware of the seven components that should be factored into all decisions, whether mundane or of major importance.

STEP 1: SMOKE OUT THE ISSUES

This may seem odd, but the first thing to do when making a decision is to decide whether the decision is even necessary! Many decisions need not even be made. This is not to say that by procrastinating, most decisions will simply vanish. Rather, by ignoring decisions that don't have to be made, you can focus on making decisions that have a real impact on your business or personal life. "Smoking out the issues" helps you eliminate "nondecisions" early in the game, so you can better apply your precious time and energy.

If you feel that a decision must be made, ask yourself:

1. Has something happened that should not have happened, and therefore needs to be *corrected or prevented* in the future?
2. Has something happened better than expected—and you want to *keep it happening*?
3. Is something *missing* that needs to be provided, or something that you want to happen not happening?

If your situation does not involve any of these questions, chances are that no decision needs to be made (at least for the moment)! If it does, then proceed on to the next step.

STEP 2: STATE YOUR PURPOSE

Once you've smoked out the issues, you're ready to state the *Decision Purpose*, which will help you determine how your decision making fits into a larger context. This is critical, but unfortunately often is overlooked. Many people ask, "Why bother to examine our purpose when we could spend the same time looking for a solution?" or "Isn't our purpose self-evident?" This mind-set leads to "seat of the pants" decision making.

One typical problem in stating the Decision Purpose is "tunnel vision," a narrowing of perceptions that ultimately restricts the search for solutions. The more broadly you state your purpose, the wider you can cast your net for solutions. And the wider the solution net, the more likely you may find a solution tailored to your needs.

Consider how one CEO during a consulting session stated his Decision Purpose as "Determine the best way to change our organization structure." When asked why, he responded by saying, "Well, we have to restore the company to a higher level of profitability, and so one of the things we must do is change the structure."

This conviction not only limited the scope of his decision, but it presupposed that he knew the root cause of "lower profitability" to be the organizational structure. In fact, restructuring was just *one* option among many others. Once he understood the blinders he was wearing, he crossed out the Decision Purpose he had written and instead wrote, "Determine the best ways to increase organizational effectiveness as one means of restoring the company to higher profitability." This new statement would serve as a platform for exploring numerous possible solutions. (Also, as you probably recall from Chapter 1, it is more productive to define what *could* be happening versus what *is not* happening first, then do some Root Cause Analysis to pinpoint just what specific areas of organizational effectiveness need strengthening.)

Another trap to avoid is the binary "either/or" Decision Purpose statement, such as "Should we invest in an IBM system?" This kind of binary statement locks you into a "Yes (Go)" or "No (No Go)" decision, restricting your options. If you recast the Decision Purpose as "What is the best data-processing system for our needs?" you won't limit your choices. The phrasing in the Decision Purpose statement should broaden, not restrict, the relevant kinds of opportunities available to you (unless you purposely want to limit your range of options to a certain number or category).

STEP 3: SET CRITERIA

Once you've "smoked out" the issues and have crafted a Decision Purpose, you're ready to determine what it is you want to *Achieve, Preserve,* and *Avoid* through your decision. Whether you realize it or not, you're always thinking in terms of these criteria; they form the basis of all decisions in life.

For instance, have you ever been driving in traffic when another car suddenly pulls out in front of you? In those few seconds, you were probably thinking, "*Achieve* a safe stop," "*Preserve* everyone's safety," and "*Avoid* hitting any object."

By elevating those criteria to a conscious level, you significantly raise the probability of selecting the best option. Consider the case of Sandy, a marketing executive who finally recognized he would have to terminate Eric, a subordinate with whom he was personally quite friendly. Sandy had never made a habit of socializing with subordinate managers, but in this instance they belonged to the same country club and played golf together.

Over time, Sandy had reached the conclusion that Eric was not really capable of performing his function. At the same time, the company had experienced a downturn and needed to cut back on its workforce. This brought Sandy to the realization that there was no other position that Eric could appropriately hold, and he would have to terminate him.

Sandy stated his Decision Purpose as "The best way to communicate to Eric my intention to terminate him." His "off-the-top-of-the-head" list included:

1. Minimize hurting his feelings.
2. Avoid misinforming him of my rationale for terminating him.
3. Minimize the damage to my personal relationship with him.
4. Avoid focusing on him as a person, rather than on the termination actions.
5. Avoid a Lose/Lose situation.
6. Avoid damaging his chances of landing a job with another company.
7. Avoid making him look bad in front of peers.
8. Avoid negative repercussions or bad "press" in the division.
9. Avoid a possible lawsuit.

You can track Sandy's thought process through the sequence of the "Avoids" he jotted down. Initially, you sense that he was quite preoccupied with the damage the termination would cause to his friendship with Eric; the fact that he actually hadn't jotted down a single "Achieve" demonstrates how concerned he was about communicating the bad news. Once he "worked through" the personal aspect of the situation, he began focusing on business issues.

In your own analysis, it's important to distinguish between "What's" and "How's" (i.e., "What" to avoid or minimize versus "How" to avoid or minimize a situation, and "What" to achieve versus "How" to achieve it); otherwise, you'll wind up with a lot of redundant objectives.

If you're not sure, apply the following test question to each of the nine "Avoids": Does this item describe what you want to avoid or minimize? Or perhaps is it a *way* of avoiding a problem you don't want to create? In Sandy's case, even though item 4, "Avoid focusing on him as a person, rather than on the termination actions," is stated as an objective, it really represents a way (or how) Sandy thinks he should conduct the termination discussion.

Comparing items 1, "Minimize hurting his feelings" and 3, "minimize the damage to my personal relationship with him," you can see that 1 is a way of accomplishing 3 and therefore is redundant.

Sandy also recognized that he'd been too avoidance focused and decided to "turn the coin over" and see if he could make an opportunity out of any of these avoidance situations. "What is it I really would like to achieve here?" he asked himself, and proceeded to develop the following list:

1. Achieve Eric's understanding of the situation and why he is being terminated.
2. Preserve my good personal relationship with him.

3. Achieve his recognition that it is the situation and his performance that is the issue, not he as a person.
4. Achieve a Win/Win situation.
5. Achieve fair termination and reference terms.
6. Preserve credibility with his peers.
7. Achieve division understanding.

As Sandy looked at this second cut of possible criteria, he felt much better about it. It was a considerably more constructive list—there were five "Achieves" in place of nine "Avoids" and "Minimizes." This suggested to him that now he'd be able to think more positively about his impending task. Already, in his mind he was starting to evaluate which of the criteria were more important when he caught himself and looked at them once again to see if there was any further redundancy or ambiguity.

This pass revealed two examples of ambiguity. For one thing, trying to achieve a Win/Win situation was too ambiguous; what he really wanted was a Win/Win/Win resolution—for the company, for Eric, and for Sandy. (It wasn't only Eric's credibility that might be at stake with his peers; Sandy's own credibility could be on the line if there was strong feeling that Eric had been unfairly treated and that his boss had made a bad judgment.)

This suggested to Sandy that items 6 and 7 could best be expressed by 7 itself, "Achieve division understanding," because both his and Eric's credibility would be preserved if items 1, 4 (now stated as "Achieve a Win/Win/Win situation), 5, and 7 were all attained.

Sandy was then able to develop a final set of criteria, which made the task ahead seem even easier.

1. Achieve Eric's understanding of the situation and why he is being terminated.
2. Achieve Eric's recognition that performance is the issue, not his personality or personal issues.

3. Achieve a Win/Win/Win resolution to the situation.
4. Achieve fair termination and reference terms.
5. Achieve division understanding.
6. Preserve my good personal relationship with him.

Sandy left item 5, "Achieve division understanding," on the list because there would probably be ways ("How's") of achieving this over and above those used to achieve the five other criteria.

In the end, the dialogue went well. By getting Eric's perceptions of his own performance before Sandy gave his feedback, Sandy could obtain a clear picture of Eric's mind-set and expectations and conduct a much more productive discussion that met his decision criteria than if he had immediately told Eric he was being terminated and the reasons why.

Eric found employment elsewhere, there were no repercussions in the company, and the two maintained a cordial relationship.

Sandy was successful partly because he used a number of techniques to refine his criteria. Eliminating redundancies was a key tool. For example, if two of your criteria are to "Achieve minimum disruption of agency services" and "Avoid demoralizing agency staff," any demoralization of the staff might cause disruption in the delivery and effectiveness of the agency services. So it's best to combine them into "Achieve minimum disruption of agency services."

Also, flip the coin over on negatively expressed criteria, translating any negatives (Avoids) into positives (Achieves) if you truly want to achieve a positive result. Remember, the best criteria are positive—they seek not only to avoid a problem or resolve a crisis but to capitalize on a situation.

Finally, as you look at your newly created list of criteria, you may also want to look back at Step 1, Smoke Out the Issues, and see if you can add anything to your list from the issues that you might subconsciously have left out the first time. The idea is to make your list as comprehensive as possible.

Write down all the criteria that occur to you, whether they're analytically derived or from your feelings. Don't be concerned if some of your criteria initially appear redundant or contradictory—you can refine them later and weed out inconsistencies. After all, if you omit an important criterion, the solution you eventually choose may be less apt to achieve your purpose.

STEP 4: SET PRIORITIES

We've just seen how powerful the words *Achieve, Preserve,* and *Avoid* can be in finding solutions to problems. Consider an age-old quandary so many companies in the financial services and insurance industries face: encouraging brokers and agents to recommend sales opportunities to their peers in other branches in other parts of the country. Typically, the reward system does not support this kind of behavior; you are rewarded for what you yourself sell, and the communication time and paperwork it often takes to refer customers or prospects to other regions is viewed by so many brokers and agents as detracting from their primary purpose of building their own sales revenues.

A major wholesale brokerage insurance company, formed several years earlier through a merger of six previously independent companies, grappled unsuccessfully with this issue for a long time, trying various organizational restructurings. Finally, a new senior vice-president of marketing and sales gathered together his regional managers and, with the full participation of the tough-minded chief financial officer, asked a key question: "What are all the things we would like to achieve, preserve, and avoid to motivate and reward our brokers and agents to refer customers or prospects to other regions or divisions?"

After some discussion, they agreed that the most creative and practical solution should:

1. Achieve a Win/Win result for all parties involved.
2. Accelerate the sale.
3. Achieve simplified accounting and recordkeeping.
4. Motivate larger contract sales.
5. Achieve strengthened branch officer interaction.
6. Demonstrate to customers that the six companies were now truly functioning as one team and represented continuity, stability, and reliability.
7. Minimize costs.
8. Avoid loss of brokers and broker support.

After ranking these and then evaluating a range of possible options, the group decided that the best incentive strategy would be twofold.

1. On all contracts under $100,000, leave it up to the involved brokers to negotiate among themselves how the commission should be split.
2. For all contracts $100,000 and over, both (or the two primary) brokers would each receive full credit for the sale.

This solution met many of the company's criteria. Even from a "Minimize costs" viewpoint, it was felt that although, in and of itself, the approach would probably *add* to costs, it was nevertheless a Win/Win arrangement that would motivate brokers to strive to obtain contracts over $100,000. The benefits of encouraging larger contracts, and indeed higher sales volume, would more than offset the increased incremental cost. This is just what has been happening since the strategy was implemented.

The insurance company was able to develop a working solution to its problem because it worked with the criteria that stood out as being more important than others. You should take the same approach with problems you are trying to solve. After completing your list of criteria in Step 3, certain issues should stand out in your mind as being more important than others. This is the time to begin setting priorities. You may want to make an initial rough cut and rate each criterion in terms of "High," "Medium," or "Low." If the list is extensive, focus on the "High's." Then ask yourself, "Are any of these items on the list [or in your mind, especially the "High's"] *absolutely necessary* for us to achieve, preserve, or avoid?" In other words, what would be the serious consequences if certain criteria were *not* met by following a particular decision path?

For example, let's say you want to buy a new computer system for your office. The amount of money you can spend may be an *Absolute Requirement*. You may say to yourself, "I will not look at any computer system [any 'option,' in the terminology of this method] that can't meet the Absolute Requirement of costing 'no more than $12,000.' " In setting an Absolute Requirement, it's necessary to have an absolute minimum level of performance required, or an absolute ceiling on the amount of any resource available (i.e., money, time, material, space, etc.). After all, there's no point in considering options that will not, at the very least, assure *minimum* satisfaction of what you're trying to achieve, preserve, or avoid. Nor is there any value to spending time evaluating and worrying about any option that will clearly cost you more than you can afford to invest in terms of time, people, money, space, equipment and material, and so forth.

It is also important to specify any Absolute Requirements in specific measurements. That way, you can evaluate each possible option against each requirement to determine whether it will indeed meet your absolute minimum standard of acceptable performance or fit within the maximum outlay of time, money, space, and so forth, you can afford to invest.

Unfortunately, few people who make decisions spend enough time differentiating sufficiently between what is *absolutely essential* and what they *ideally* would like to achieve, preserve, or avoid. Even when they think they have done this, too often their Absolute Requirements are not measurable from a practical viewpoint; for example, they'll say they must "Achieve highest profitability possible," "Minimize expenditures," or "Achieve high morale." None of these are Absolute Requirements; they're *Desirable Objectives*—the more they can be attained, the better. In contrast, Absolute Requirements are just that—absolute.

It's also important to distinguish Absolute Requirements from the Desirable Objectives you ideally want to achieve, preserve, and avoid but that are not essential to meet. Your first source of Desirable Objectives is your list of Absolute Requirements. Reflect on the Absolute Requirements and list those where you'd like to exceed the minimum requirements or spend less than the maximum amount you have available of any resource (such as for a maximum budget of $12,000 for the computer—e.g., "Minimize cost of the computer"). Those objectives that are derived from the Absolute Requirements, plus those objectives that are not absolute but remain on the original list, will be Desirable Objectives.

Rank the objectives on a 10 to 1 scale, with 10 being the most important. Use good, hard thinking at this step because the options that meet all your Absolute Requirements should also be evaluated against the Desirable Objectives in order to discriminate among them and decide which one(s) really meet your Decision Purpose.

For example, let's go back to buying that new computer system. If the most important Desirable Objective was that it should have a 200-megabyte hard drive, you might give that objective a 10. Then ask yourself which is the next most important objective—perhaps interfaceability with other systems. Now, how important is the hard drive capacity compared to the expandability? Is it half as important (in which case you'd give it a 5), or about 80 percent as important (if so, give it an 8)? Is it equally important? (If so, give it a 10.)

Table 3.1 extends this line of thinking and assigns a quantitative judgment to each objective. Note that this is not meant to reduce the rating process to a mere numbers game. Rather, the goal is to accurately express your values, feelings, and judgment about a particular decision based on the best information you can generate about the situation.

Remember that when you rate your various objectives, the better you can differentiate among them, the easier it will be to spot a true winning solution. For example, if you give all Desirable Objectives a value of 10, you will have a hard time differentiating among the options because the scores will be so close. Also, don't simply scale the objectives (say, 10 percent apart)—the goal is to create an accurate reflection of your judgment in rating each of the Desirable Objectives compared to the ones scoring 10 points. Perfect symmetry is not the objective.

STEP 5: IDENTIFY OPTIONS

After you've set your Absolute Requirements and ranked your Desirable Objectives according to their value and importance to one another, it's time to start identifying options, that is, listing all the ways that you might meet your decision criteria. The first place to look for options is your criteria list itself—many times the most innovative solutions to problems will emerge from the list of what you want to accomplish. Use your experience to derive possible options from your Absolute Requirements and Desirable Objectives.

In the previous example, Sandy placed a high value on achieving Eric's recognition, and therefore tailored his strategy to that criterion. As mentioned earlier, rather than simply telling Eric he was being terminated, he decided to explain things in the context of Eric's mind-set, so that they would be more understandable and convey as much goodwill as possible. Sandy actually developed four possible approaches to the ter-

Table 3.1 Selecting a Computer

	R	R×V	R	R×V	R	R×V
Determine the best computer system for the office.						
Absolute Requirements						
1. Maximum investment of $30,000 "installed"						
2. Must be able to have complex data analysis program custom-developed to meet employee needs						
Desirable Objectives	*Value*					
1. 200-megabyte capacity	10					
2. Achieve highest quality hard drive, monitor, and printer within maximum price	8					

	Weight								
3. Achieve maximum software capacity (using a variety of software, including word processing, accounting, database, graphic design, and desktop publishing)	8								
4. Achieve best interface ability with other computers in office	7								
5. Achieve most affordable software	6								
6. Interface with other computers in other businesses	5								
7. Achieve low learning curve; easy to use	4								
8. Minimize cost of network interfacing	4								
9. Avoid high maintenance and repair costs	3								
10. Minimize total investment	2								

mination interview and selected the "mind-set" approach that best fit his decision criteria.

To return to the computer purchase example, following are some potential options:

1. Stay with your current system.
2. Upgrade your current system.
3. Buy a new, Brand A system.

STEP 6: TEST YOUR OPTIONS AGAINST YOUR CRITERIA

Once you have a list with which you're comfortable, it's time to start testing your options against your criteria. For a complex decision with a number of Absolute Requirements and Desirable Objectives, it's helpful to set up a matrix format that lists your Absolute Requirements and Desirable Objectives in the left column, and your options along the top. (See Table 3.2.)

Decide for each cell in the matrix whether the option satisfies every Absolute Requirement (if any exists). As soon as an option fails to meet even one minimum requirement or exceeds the ceiling on the amount of any available resource, shoot it down. If an option is questionable in terms of meeting

Table 3.2 Evaluating Options

	Option 1	*Option 2*	*Option 3*
Absolutely must meet these requirements:			
Desirable Objectives:			

any Absolute Requirements, you'd better get more data before adopting it; otherwise, you may choose an option that violates an essential decision criterion.

If you've made your best judgments based on the best information available to you and one or more options meet all the Absolute Requirements, then your analysis is indicating that this (or any of these options) should satisfy at least the minimum requirements of the situation. Now the task is to select the one(s) that will do the best job for you.

Any options that have successfully survived your testing against each Absolute Requirement can now be evaluated against your Desirable Objectives. Ask, "Based on the best available information I have about each option relative to this first Desirable Objective, which one does the best job?"

Once you've selected the option that does the best job on any given Desirable Objective, write down why it does so under that option and opposite that Desirable Objective. Also, give that option a 10. Then go on to your other options and ask, "Which of these remaining options does the next best job of meeting the first objective?" Again, write down why it does so well or so poorly under its column opposite the objective in question. Then give the option a relative value in terms of how well it satisfies the objective compared with your first option. (An option that does only half as well by comparison with your 10 only gets a 5, and so on.) Even if none of the options does a superior job of meeting the Desirable Objective, by all means give the best one a 10 and factor the others downward.

Next, move down to the second most Desirable Objective and do the same thing. Keep repeating this process until you've finished ranking all the options that met the Absolute Requirements in terms of how well they meet the Desirable Objectives.

After you've finished ranking all the options against the Desirable Objectives, multiply all the option scores (the ratings, or R's) against the values of the Desirable Objectives (the V's—see Table 3.3). This score takes into account the relative

Table 3.3 Selecting the Best Computer System

Determine the best computer system for the office.*	Value	Keep the current (CPT) system	R	R×V	Buy Brand A (Macintosh)	R	R×V	Buy Brand B (IBM)	R	R×V
Criteria										
Absolute Requirements										
1. Maximum investment of $30,000 "installed"		Yes			Yes			Yes		
2. Must be able to have complex data analysis program custom-developed to meet employee needs		Yes			Yes			Yes		
Desirable Objectives										
1. 200-megabyte capacity	10	Maximum 50 megabyte	3	27	200+ megabyte capacity	10	90	200+ megabyte capacity	10	90
2. Achieve highest quality hard drive, monitor, and printer within maximum price	8	Very poor. System is old. Poor-quality printing	1	10	Best possible printing, excellent hard drives	10	100	Excellent hard drives but lesser quality printers	8	80
3. Achieve maximum software capacity (using a variety of software, including word processing, accounting, database, graphic design, and desktop publishing)	8	No, integrates with no other software	0	0	Excellent range of software interfacing	10	80	Good range of software capacity	6	48
4. Achieve best interface ability with other computers in office	7	Slow and cumbersome	3	21	Excellent network	10	70	Excellent network	10	70
5. Achieve most affordable software	6	N/A	0	0	Wide variety available at competitive prices	10	60	Database software is more expensive than the computer	2	12

64

Criteria	Weight									
6. Interface with other computers in other businesses	5	1	No one else is using this system	5	5	Will interface, but most companies use Brand B —may require a translator	25	10	Interfaces easily and is the industry standard	50
7. Achieve low learning curve; easy to use	4	2	Very difficult and needs specialized training	8	10	Easiest to learn; little to no experience required	40	6	Complex, but many people know Brand B	24
8. Minimize cost of network interfacing	4	0	N/A	0	8	Competitive (even if requiring translators)	32	10	Competitive	40
9. Avoid high maintenance and repair costs	3	4	Parts difficult and slow to come by	12	10	More competitive maintenance contracts	30	8	Less competitive maintenance contracts	24
10. Minimize total investment	2	2	Training of personnel is quite expensive	4	10	Little to no investment for training	20	6	Some training required	12
Totals				87			547			450

*Note: One theoretical option, "Upgrade the current (CPT) system," is not included in this evaluation. It was discovered that the current computer system was at the limit of its technology and could not be upgraded.

importance of each Desirable Objective times how well each option met that Desirable Objective.

Finally, add the totals for each option to determine which option does the best overall job of meeting the Desirable Objectives, which is second best, and so forth.

If one of the options scores 15 percent or higher than the others, it tentatively is the best choice. Following is an evaluation of computers against the criteria described in Table 3.1. In this computer example, the choice of buying Brand A is about 18 percent better than Brand B, so it exceeds the 15 percent guideline. Brand A, however, did not do particularly well on Objective 6, "Interface with other computers in other businesses," scoring only half as well as Brand B. But that objective was only valued a 5, so this is not a serious liability. Sometimes you can strengthen an option by combining it with a quality of another, less satisfactory option that did indeed score well on the criterion in question. Just be sure to factor in any additional resources required so you're sure that the benefits still outweigh the costs!

Based on your numerical analysis, you can choose a tentative winner (i.e., the one or more options that meet any and all Absolute Requirements and that best serve the Desirable Objectives). If your gut feeling says that it isn't the right choice, though, go back and look at the comparison of options to see where it did and didn't do well. You may, in fact, come out with a clearer picture of the situation, either because of the closeness of the scores of several options (within 15 percent of each other) or because of your discomfort level.

Finally, ask yourself if, by looking at the weak points in your tentative winners, you can find ways to strengthen them at all. If this happens, go back to your options to determine which one(s) did the best job of fulfilling the criteria that the winner didn't satisfy well. Try to take the best characteristics from one or more of these options to form a new, creative option that may score even better than your winner—one that in your judgment does not have any (or as many) inherent vulnerabilities.

If there are any additional resource costs involved with the new option—money, time, space, equipment, and so forth—then factor the new data into the matrix and rescore the option accordingly against the others to be sure that the additional benefits still outweigh the additional costs! It is also wise to check all of your criteria to test whether you still agree with the judgments you made about each and, of course, the validity of the data on the options that you judged.

Here's what to ask, in either case:

1. Did you state your *purpose* correctly—is it broad enough?
2. Are there any additional *criteria* that need to be achieved, preserved, or avoided that you failed to state?
3. Are your *Absolute Requirements* truly essential, and the maximums and minimums mandatory?
4. Looking at the values you assigned to the *Desirable Objectives*, do they accurately reflect your priorities now?
5. Have you overlooked any other *options* that deserve consideration?
6. Are you confident of the accuracy and completeness of the data you used to rate your options, especially against the highly valued *Desirable Objectives*?
7. Do the scores you assigned to the options accurately reflect your best judgment?
8. Did you use a 10 high rating for the option that best satisfied each Desirable Objective, and rank the others downward in ratio accordingly?
9. Are there any serious holes in the best options as you look at them against the high-priority Desirable Objective?
10. Could you combine one or more options, especially in areas where the tentative winner is weak and another is strong?
11. Did you make any arithmetic errors?

STEP 7: TROUBLESHOOT AND REFINE YOUR CHOICE

The last step in the decision process is to troubleshoot and refine your decision. Ask yourself not only "How can the winner be further improved?" but also "What could go wrong with the communication and implementation of my choice?"—a topic that paves the way for the third part of the *Complete Thought Process*: Risk Analysis. (See Part III of this book.)

THE FIVE-MINUTE DECISION MAKER

At this point, you might be thinking, "That's an awful lot to go through to evaluate a decision and make a choice." At first, it *is* a lot of work. But if you use the system to make a decision that could lead to millions of dollars in gain or loss, or that has significant human consequences, isn't it worth the time to ensure that you'll make the right choice? Also, as you get better at using the system, you'll walk through the steps automatically, so that it becomes a more natural mental process.

To illustrate how quickly the decision-making system can actually be used, take a look at the following example, which applies Option Analysis to the (sometimes) simple act of buying a special birthday present for a friend.

Happy Birthday!

Your best friend is about to turn 40, and you want to purchase something special to commemorate the event. Start with Step 1, Smoke out the issues. The issue is obvious: Your friend is having a special birthday. Still, get into the habit of jotting down even "obvious" issues; eventually, you'll deal with a problem in which the issues are not what they appear on the surface, or they may be obstructed from view altogether.

Now move on to Step 2, State your purpose. That's easy enough in this case: to select the best present for your best friend's 40th birthday. Again, jot it down—you're trying to make Option Analysis an automatic process, so don't cut corners while you're learning the steps.

Let's go on to Step 3, Set criteria. What do you want to achieve, preserve, and avoid by purchasing the present? (We'll look at some samples in a moment.)

Step 4 is to set priorities on the criteria you listed in the previous step. Are there any Absolute Requirements? For example, there's probably a maximum amount of money you can afford to spend on the gift. Or, when must the gift arrive? What about desirable criteria? Do you want the gift to be something that's enjoyed and consumed or treasured forever?

The next step entails identifying options: What are all the possible gifts you want to consider that you think could at least meet the Absolute Requirements (and do a pretty good job of meeting your Desirable Objectives)? Once you've listed your options, set them up in a matrix format and start Step 6, Test your options against your criteria. (See Table 3.4.)

If an option meets the first Absolute Requirement, put a checkmark under it and keep going; if it doesn't, shoot it down on the spot (by placing an "X" under it) and go on to evaluate the next possible gift on your list. (See Table 3.5.) Then, test those options that meet every single Absolute Requirement against any Desirable Objectives. As you compare these options, ask yourself, "Which does the best job of meeting the first Desirable Objective?" Give that gift two checkmarks. (See Table 3.6.)

Are there any others that do almost as well in meeting that Objective? If so, give them just one checkmark. Continue this for each Desirable Objective. The birthday gift with the most checkmarks wins, as long as you cannot identify any highly serious pitfalls with it (Step 7), and it meets every Absolute Requirement. And the winner is: the hammock.

Time: about 3 to 5 minutes.

Table 3.4 Determine the Best Birthday Present

Issue: The best present for Clyde's birthday	1. Expensive Bottle of Champagne	2. Hammock	3. Picture Frame	4. A "Fun" Weekend Somewhere	5. Radar Detector	6. Puppy
Absolutely must, without fail:						
1. Cost under $150						
2. Be deliverable no later than May 11						
In addition, it should:						
3. Be unusual						
4. Be something to use/relax with						
5. Last for a few years						
6. Be something his wife will also enjoy						
Total						

Table 3.5 The Best Birthday Present (Absolute Requirements)

Issue: The best present for Clyde's birthday	1. Expensive Bottle of Champagne	2. Hammock	3. Picture Frame	4. A"Fun" Weekend Somewhere	5. Radar Detector	6. Puppy
Absolutely must, without fail:						
1. Cost under $150	✓	✓	✓	X	Poor quality but just under $150	✓
2. Be deliverable no later than May 11	✓	✓	✓		✓	X

71

Table 3.6 The Best Birthday Present (Desirable Objectives)

In addition, it should:	1. Expensive Bottle of Champagne	2. Hammock	3. Picture Frame	4. A"Fun" Weekend Somewhere	5. Radar Detector	6. Puppy
3. Be unusual	✓✓	✓✓	✓			
4. Be something to use/relax with	✓✓	✓✓				
5. Last for a few years		✓✓	✓		✓	
6. Be something his wife will also enjoy		✓✓				
Total		**WINNER**				

Code: ✓✓ = "Best"
   ✓ = "Good"
   X = "Shot down" and so ruled out of further consideration.

72

ONWARD

Chapters 4 through 8 show Option Analysis in action on the corporate battlefield. When you're done with Chapter 8, you'll be ready to add a new dimension to your decision-making process: Risk Analysis. Risk Analysis is the final component of the *Complete Thought Process*, and it answers the question: "What are the downsides (and possible upsides) of going with the option you have selected as the winner?" We'll worry about that later on. For now, read on so you can see Option Analysis in a variety of real-world contexts and can better apply it to your own life.

CHAPTER FOUR

Option Analysis in Action—1: Trouble South of the Border

Since the late 1800s, Americon Inc., headquartered in the southeastern United States, has been a major producer of specialty bulk chemicals and related consumer products. Though successful at both businesses, for at least 20 years senior management had argued about whether the company should primarily be a chemical or a consumer company. Although the specialty chemical segment of the business was far more profitable, it was not nearly as glamorous as the consumer products division, and it didn't offer the same kind of breakaway potential. Rivalry between the two divisions ran high, which in turn made it difficult for management of the two divisions to agree on decisions that benefited the company as a whole. Somehow, the company had to adopt a decision-making system that would make everyone a winner.

Davis, president of the Chemicals Division, often found himself fiercely competing against the Consumer Division for scarce resources. Unfortunately for him, the Consumer Division generally won the lion's share of moneys earmarked for new investments. This had become more the rule than the exception, and Davis questioned whether there was a significant growth opportunity for him with Americon and was considering looking elsewhere. So it was with some degree of pessimism that he presented a recommendation to the board of directors that Americon invest an additional $3.5 million in a specialty plant based in Brazil. Americon owned a 49 percent stake in the plant, which manufactured a chemical used in television screens to reduce electromagnetic emissions. The raw material for the chemical was mined in Brazil, and with the trend toward larger TV screens, which needed significantly more of the chemical than smaller screens, the worldwide market potential was enormous.

The only glitch Davis could see was that the capacity of the Brazilian plant was insufficient to meet the market potential. Unfortunately, despite the best research that Davis presented, the majority Brazilian owner refused to consider the expansion; the company was attempting to build up its own asset base in Brazil and expense everything it could of its capital plant equipment, rather than running it run through its P&L. Americon's own Board of Directors was also reluctant; so far, the Brazilian plant had not performed up to Davis's plan, despite the $2.5 million Americon had already pumped into the operation. Also, if the opportunity was so significant, the board wondered why the Brazilian partner continued to refuse to fund the expansion. Not surprisingly, the board rejected Davis' recommendation.

The morning following the board meeting, Davis and Americon's CEO, Edward Wendt, sat rather disconsolately reviewing their failure to win the board's approval. After a period of silence, Davis suddenly said, "You know, Ed, maybe we should step backward and take into account the concerns expressed by the board—let's use Option Analysis and see if we come up with any creative alternatives that none of us have thought about." (Both men had participated in a recent Americon management committee project in which they learned how to use the Option Analysis method and had successfully applied it to several crucial company concerns.)

Wendt readily agreed, saying, "Well, at this point I guess it wouldn't hurt. Maybe we would gain something after all. I suppose we might as well give it a try. Who else do you think ought to work with us in thinking through the situation?"

Davis rattled off a list of the appropriate senior managers, including: the senior vice president for sales and marketing; the Chemicals Division general manager and the product manager for the particular specialty chemical, the vice-president of R&D, the vice-president of operations, the director of market research, the head of purchasing, the chief financial officer, and the legal counsel.

In order to avoid unduly influencing this management group by virtue of his position, Wendt suggested that Davis conduct the meeting—not as a "pitch" man, but as a chairperson.

Two days later the group convened, and Davis began by reviewing the process for the benefit of those who had not participated in the corporate management committee project. He asked if a decision was really necessary. Everyone concurred, so he went on to Step 2, State your purpose, and asked, "What is it we're trying to determine?"

The director of market research, Bill Calvin, immediately suggested an answer. "That's easy," he said. "We need to figure out how to convince the board that we do have a window of opportunity with this product and now is the time to make an investment that will help us significantly boost our market share."

Davis picked up a marking pen and went to the electronic copy board. He began writing down people's answers.

"On the contrary," countered Ted Glass, the chief financial officer. "We're trying to determine whether we should even be in partnership with our Brazilian colleagues. Their objective seems to be to squeeze everything they can out of us—they certainly haven't followed through on their commitments to us."

Sarah Finch, the head of purchasing, then suggested, "Why don't we look for another joint venture partner to come in with us and buy out some portion of the Brazilian's ownership stake? We would then have the majority ownership and reduce our financial risk accordingly."

Jake Winthrop, the legal counsel for the division, immediately mentioned several factors having to do with Brazilian laws that would prohibit anyone but the Brazilian company having majority ownership. Davis also pointed out that the suggestion of finding a third partner was really Step 5 of the Decision Process, Identify options, and that it would be more efficient to first resolve their discussion about Step 2—"What is it we're really trying to determine?"—and then set and agree on criteria (Step 3). Then they could get into suggestions on what they might or might not consider doing.

Kathryn Kettle, the senior vice president of sales and marketing, then asked, "Aren't we really concerned with finding the best way to capitalize on this international market opportunity?"

CEO Ed Wendt directed his question to Ted Glass: "Aren't there some things we could do to dress up the operation with minimal investment that wouldn't require the board's approval and then convince some prospective buyer to pay $4 or $5 million for this? After all, there's such an excellent market opportunity; there must be other companies that could capitalize on this and yet wouldn't represent too great a competitive threat to us."

"That's just the problem," said Kathryn Kettle. "I think it could give someone a competitive edge in certain product niches. It could enable them to shoehorn their way in, and then they could leverage their opportunity from there against us. For example, our number one European competitor who . . ."

"Hey, hold on, people," interrupted Davis. "You're off the track again. I thought we agreed we weren't going to talk about whether we should do this or do that because we just get into a seesaw battle of ideas. Let's just focus on what we really need to determine. Then, once we agree on that, we'll go on to the next step and decide on a set of criteria that we all agree should be met by whatever is the best thing to do in this situation."

"I guess you're right," said Ed Wendt. "We're going around the mulberry bush time and again. I guess it does make sense to try to be a little more disciplined and stick to the process. In fact, I don't necessarily think that what we're trying to determine is any of the items that have been suggested! I've been thinking about this situation for a couple of days now, and I wonder if maybe we should be taking a much broader look at the situation. What I have in mind as our purpose is this: to determine what's the best thing we should do regarding our 49 percent ownership relationship."

The group nodded in agreement with Wendt's suggestion, and Davis continued the process. "Let's develop our criteria by asking, 'What do we want to *achieve, preserve,* and *avoid*?' "

"Well, the very first thing I think we must achieve," spoke up Kathryn Kettle, "is that whatever we do, we cannot risk any injury whatsoever to our trademark and image, at least in the United States."

"I certainly agree with that," affirmed Ted Glass. Several other heads nodded assent. Davis wrote down the suggestion on the copy board, "Avoid any adverse impact on our trademark and image," as he commented, "Let's postpone discussion of whether it is an Absolute Requirement until we get to the next step."

Davis then summarized on the copyboard what he recalled of the dialogue thus far.

- Capitalize on the "window of opportunity."
- Reduce our risk.
- Avoid giving someone a competitive edge on us.

General manager Charles Gibbs spoke up: "I agree that we want to capitalize on the market opportunity available to us.

But you need to add 'in many parts of the world' and 'as soon as possible.'"

"Right," responded Davis as he quickly wrote these two suggestions down. "What else?"

"We'd better make sure whatever we do doesn't antagonize our Brazilian partner or whatever choice we make is bound to fail," suggested Leonard King, the vice-president of operations.

"Darn right," said Ted Glass. "Although I wouldn't mind scaring them a little since I feel we've been used and abused by them to some extent."

"How about turning that into a positive?" suggested Wendt. "Whatever we decide to do, it should be motivating to our Brazilian partner."

"Yep. I can't disagree with that," said Glass.

"Are there any other criteria?" asked Davis.

Interestingly enough, after they had finished their discussion and agreed on a total list of nine criteria, and Davis had asked if there were truly any absolutely essential requirements, only one fell in that category: "Do nothing that will risk injuring our trademark and image in the United States." The remaining criteria were all Desirable Objectives and were weighted accordingly, in ratio to one another. But none of these was seen as essential.

Next, under Davis's direction, the group generated a list of options to be considered:

1. Continue as is.
2. Invest another $1.5 million after somehow convincing the Brazilian partner to do the same.
3. Entice a European or Japanese company in the business to make the necessary investment, reducing our ownership and thereby sharing the risk and reward, ensuring that we then can build the additional capacity to meet the projected sales potential.
4. Either now or at some point in the future, sell our per-

centage of ownership and get out of Brazil (and indeed the business).

In two 4-hour sessions—separated by several days during which the group members gathered information on each option in terms of the criteria they had established earlier—they completed their analysis. And since they were motivated by a common purpose, had agreed on specifications for the decision, and had participated in applying an explicit decision-making process, they all agreed that option 3 best suited their immediate objective, with the possible longer-term goal of divesting their ownership completely (option 4).

By enticing another company in the business to purchase partial ownership of the Brazilian plant, buying some of Americon's shares and some of the Brazilian partner's shares, they thought they could convince the Brazilian partner to join them in making the necessary investment to expand plant capacity. At the same time, the Brazilian partner could use the balance of the funding to add to its own asset base and reduce its own risk in the plant.

Ideally, the joint venture partner would be another specialty chemical company that exported heavily to the United States and the Far East, particularly to Japan, but did not have the right product for use in the manufacture of the new large TV screens.

Davis's group quickly selected the best potential partner (a European chemical maker), and within 3 months had succeeded in putting together a deal that met with enthusiasm on the part of Americon's board and the Brazilian partner. By Brazilian law, the Brazilian firm had to be the majority owner—34 percent in this case. Americon and the European firm each held a 33 percent interest.

A year later, given a shift in its strategic objectives, Americon was able to implement the fourth option, selling its shares to both companies so that the Brazilian company went back to its 51 percent ownership and the European competitor increased its holdings to 49 percent. According to Davis, "We got out of the business, making a 37 percent return on our investment over the 3-year period. This was viewed as a tremendous success in our company both by operating management and by the board of directors, especially since we had been way under plan. And the Europeans were pleased—while they were a minority partner to the Brazilians, they were able to insist on some strong clauses in the legal agreement which, in effect, gave them 50 percent voting rights and, therefore, more equal control of the company. So it was a win for the Brazilians, a win for the Europeans, and certainly a win for us!"

Davis's handling of this decision-making session, his management of the negotiations with the Europeans and the Brazilians, his handling of the joint venture partner relationship, and his coordinating the eventual sale of their minority ownership all raised his stature in the eyes of CEO Wendt and the board of directors. Also, because he contributed valuable ideas to the consumer products division that helped strengthen its sales and profitability, Davis was given additional responsibilities for several consumer product lines. This broadened his own technical knowledge and management skills, and helped break down the competitive feelings between the company's two main divisions. Davis, by the way, dropped all thoughts of interviewing elsewhere—how could he possibly have time with all the satisfying work he had to do?

* * *

The preceding application of Option Analysis brings up a number of important points that you should keep in mind.

1. Option Analysis is a dynamic process; you might arrive at an immediate "best" option that will give way to another option in the future. This is what happened in the Americon situation. The best immediate option was

to bring in a partner (option 3), with the ultimate hope of divesting its shares altogether in the future (option 4).

The best option is one that meets *all* your Absolute Requirements and does the best job on the Desirable Objectives, with no significant gaps. As in this application of Option Analysis, the best decision proved to be a combination of two options—one for the immediate future and one for the long term.

2. Wherever there is competition for scarce resources—be they for money, time, material, equipment, space, and so forth—it's difficult to truly achieve Win/Win/Win solutions that are in the best interests of the company or organization. Check your own experience against the following: Doesn't it often happen that one side wins and the other feels it has lost, or a compromise is reached that's really not satisfactory to either side?

In this instance, a number of people had felt in a Lose/Lose position: Davis and his group in the chemical division felt they were shot down by the board of directors, and that as a result they, as well as the company, were losing an important opportunity; at the same time, if the board had agreed to fund the $3.5 million, the consumer products managers would have felt that they had indirectly "lost," because that money would not have been available for their projects. The Option Analysis, and Davis's performance, resulted in a way to resolve the conflict between the two divisions.

3. It's important to be realistic about who needs to be involved in doing the Option Analysis and how much time it may take. Many companies make the mistake of not involving people whose input—and especially buy-in to any eventual decision—is truly relevant to the process. Another mistake is for the chairperson, consciously or unconsciously, to "stack the deck," loading the room

with people who favor his or her position. This, of course, will lead to a biased answer and possibly the wrong decision. In this instance, Davis held back from promulgating his own views and filled the Option Analysis *guardian* role exceedingly well.

4. It's often difficult for the president or key executive who truly wants the professional objectivity of his or her managers to lead such an analysis and discussion if there is in fact a predetermined preferred outcome. In such instances, it's important either to turn over the role of chairperson to someone with sufficient training in the process to lead the group, or to follow the remaining steps in the process faithfully to prevent a favored solution from filtering out other alternatives that could prove to be far better ones for the organization.

   If objective leadership for the process can't be found, you might consider bringing in an external resource to function as a catalyst. The catalyst is there not only to lead the discussion, but to add value from his or her own practitioner experience.

   There are many other advantages to this practice, an important one being that the executive does not have to wear both the *process* and the *content* hats, but can focus increasingly on the people who are grappling with the issue. In this way, the executive can judge who is really a team player, who seems to have the organization's interest truly at heart, who's playing it "close to the vest," who's competing with others in the room, who is parochial in outlook, who is highly conceptual, who is a good communicator, and so forth. This can be invaluable information, especially to a new chief executive or other manager who is newly promoted or appointed to a task force.

5. The more complex and polarized the issue, the more benefit there is to bringing an external resource to func-

tion as the catalyst. As noted previously, the catalyst is there not only to lead the discussion, but to add value from his or her own experience.

6. It's important to recognize that, just as one needs to look out of both eyes to get an accurate picture of the world, one needs to be equally concerned in decision making with both the *process* being used and the *content* or substance of the issue being discussed.

7. Its important to balance *process* and *content*. If the *process* is ignored, chances are that the discussion will involve a good deal of argumentation and possibly result in a poor decision. But by focusing too strongly on the process, people may become too concerned with their impact on others and not focus sufficiently on the substantive issues and information. Here again is where it's important to have someone familiar with Option Analysis who can function as a practitioner.

8. Davis used an electronic copy board (an electronic easel that makes copies on the spot). But if a copy board isn't available, use easels and chart paper, or a blackboard. You may also wish to have a "note taker" sitting in with a PC or a laptop computer. When the milestones of the process have been reached, the copy board or note taker prints out results, and you can distribute copies to each member. (This enables the group to really focus on incremental pieces of the puzzle as well as the macro viewpoint. Also, the focus on applying the group's best professional thinking and judgment to a critical issue, while quickly distilling, copying, editing, and reaching agreement on the judgments taken—accelerates the entire decision process, raising the probability of a higher-quality decision.)

Group members can edit the notes as appropriate and buy in to the finished product (i.e., the decision with its complete analysis for presentation to senior management, customers, the board of directors, investment analysts, etc.). It also facilitates building esprit de corps and teamwork, which generally means greater commitment and follow-through execution so that the decision has the best chance of being implemented properly, achieving its purpose (Step 2) and satisfying each of the criteria and priorities (Steps 3 and 4).

CHAPTER FIVE

$$\text{OOO}$$

Option Analysis in Action—2: The Glue Factory

"By this acquisition, we will further strengthen our position in the worldwide light industrial equipment market by acquiring the assets of Kenderson, the world's largest manufacturer of hydraulics. As this industry is adjusting to worldwide market conditions, the trend has been toward stronger, vertically integrated manufacturers. This acquisition will help us compete vigorously in more segments of the industry, especially since the product line and dealer organizations of the two businesses fit together extremely well.

"No immediate changes are contemplated for the operations, manufacturing facilities, or existing dealer organizations. If, over the long term, changes occur, they will be made only after the needs of our customers, dealers, and employees are fully considered.

"This acquisition will give the business combined annual sales of more than $2 billion, 18,000 employees, and sales outlets in more than 100 countries."

So announced the press release from Darco Corporation. The release went on to describe Kenderson, including its worldwide assets, its wholesale receivables, its facilities in a dozen countries, and its trademarks.

In any transaction of this type amounting to half a billion dollars or more, and particularly when buying a competitor, there invariably are a number of strong cultural contrasts that must be carefully identified and then intelligently and sensitively managed.

In this mega-merger, interviews of 75 senior managers of each company and 20 dealers on both sides of the Atlantic Ocean revealed that there were 16 strong cultural contrasts. The major differences between the two competitors can be summed up as follows:

Darco	**Kenderson**
Short-term profit-oriented	Customer-oriented
Focus on cost/value ratio	Focus on quality
A follower on innovation	A leader in product innovation
Worldwide dealer network	Shares dealers with other manufacturers
Strong autocratic management style	Participative management
Political/rank-conscious	Warm "family" feeling
Offshore organizations controlled by U.S. headquarters	Offshore operations independent
Good planning processes	Lacks long-range planning
Highly unionized	Nonunion
Highly centralized	Decentralized structure
Salaries high for industry	Salaries low for industry

Darco President Art Lamb and his fellow senior executives concluded that a 6-day conference with key managers from Kenderson would be the best way to tackle the toughest issues and get the two companies off on the right foot, rather than waiting for clashes that would inevitably degrade performance of both companies.

The group convened at an executive retreat, but before trying to meld the two companies, Lamb and his staff sat down and used the Root Cause Analysis method in part to determine five key issues (Step 1) that had to be resolved before the companies could operate in harmony. They concluded that suitable options had to be found for the following:

1. *Direction and Strategy.* Establish a common business philosophy (goals and objectives and guiding principles). We must communicate this overall plan so that our people and dealers will have confidence in the future.
2. *Dealer Integration.* Resolve the dealer network thoughtfully and communicate the decisions. Decide whether to/when/how/where. Plan should be timed to maintain sales and customer service.
3. *Organization Structure.* Determine the policy about integration with the acquired. Resolve centralized versus decentralized structure and communicate it quickly to both our people and dealers.
4. *Human Resources Issues.* Decide and resolve critical human resources issues before we can plan and ensure early achievement of any plan to combine the marketing and sales organizations and allay current employee concerns.
5. *Strategic Planning.* Decide on future product development and strategy for becoming the industry leader. [Specific areas were given.]

With these in mind, Lamb had the top 16 executives from each of the two companies meet for a day and a half, beginning with lunch. Until this, many of the men had never met the others from the other company. To break the ice, Lamb grouped the managers into intercompany teams, who then played ten rounds of a simulation game that was designed to provide a common frame of reference for analyzing the five major issues.

Plunging these executives into the simulation before tackling the real-world dilemmas enabled them to experience how they addressed and tried to resolve issues in a safer and more experimental environment than if they immediately had to confront the complex gut issues facing them. It also gave them an opportunity to get to know one another better, have some laughs and winks together as they experienced difficulties in managing the situations presented to them by the simulation, and begin feeling more comfortable together. Finally, it enabled them to start developing some common management tools that they could then apply to their real issues and opportunities.

The simulation also revealed that many of the executives brought with them conflicting objectives. For example, some Kenderson people were convinced that there should be two organizations and very probably two distinct *Missions*; in other words, Kenderson should retain its autonomy and corporate integrity. In contrast, Darco executives felt strongly that the acquired firm should be integrated into Darco's operations.

Once some of these conflicts had been aired, the group under Lamb's leadership agreed on the following set of *Conference Objectives*:

1. Establish a jointly agreed-on *Mission Statement* for the overall businesses.
   a. One Mission or two?
   b. Differentiated Mission Statements by market?
2. Decide what are primary directions, decisions, and business strategies in major market areas of the world that the group agrees are critical to other policy determinations.
3. Decide which are the most critical dealer or distributor issues and make decisions.
   a. Rate of essential change ("crunch")?
   b. Exclusivity or dual dealers?
   c. Different dealer policies for different markets?

4. Based on conclusions under items 1, 2, and 3, determine the principal elements of organization structure.
   a. One organization or two?
   b. Product orientation or not?
   c. International or domestic?
5. Unionization: What policies can we, or should we, have with respect to unions? (Define the problem and establish a plan for resolution.) At a minimum, share information.
6. Determine which of the preceding decisions need to be communicated, by whom, and to whom, and establish a clear policy and timetable.
7. Identify additional issues from the priority issues and establish a process for their resolution, with a timetable and accountability, and with a closely monitored follow-up process.
8. In the process, develop significant esprit de corps.
9. Agree on the modus operandi for the next several months.
10. Leave the conference committed to a company plan.

When this next conference of eight senior executives from each company convened, and following a "remove the blinders/open up the opportunity lens" exercise that led to the development of a set of "ground rules," the group started right in with the first issue on the agenda—Mission and direction. Using the Option Analysis method, they began looking at the first issue: Should there be one or two Missions for Darco and Kenderson (Step 2)? After applying the Option Analysis method, the 16 executives agreed there had to be only *one* Mission.

The next decision concerned the extent to which the combined Darco–Kenderson effort should compete more aggressively in North America. To make this difficult decision, the group first agreed that it should evaluate the decision in terms of such objectives as profitability, market share, marketing strategy, customers, dealers, and employees. Under each of these areas, they developed a list of criteria (Step 3). For example, with regard to market share, several of their criteria were:

1. Achieve:
   a. Heartland market share at least equal to the rest of North America
   b. Number 3 position or get out (i.e., x percent in product line A, y percent in B, etc.)
2. Achieve number 2 position in [geographical area] by [date].
3. Achieve number 1 position against [primary competitor] in customer satisfaction in present range of [particular product line].
4. Invest and achieve minimum 5 percent real growth rank in volume each year in constant dollars.
5. Avoid actions that negatively impact [particular product lines] in other parts of the world.

Agreeing on these criteria enabled the top managers, who had entered the conference with some strongly contradictory ideas, to evaluate five basic strategies, then reach consensus on the general direction for both product and market representation in the majority of North America. Essentially, they adopted a more aggressive strategy to permeate the Heartland of North America, keeping Darco's commitment to the coastal areas at a slightly more intensified level.

Next, they applied Option Analysis to the issue of international dealer organization. This was a significant concern, since each company had its own dealership organizations worldwide, yet some dealers were dual distributors (i.e., distributors who represented both competitors) and others represented only one company. Again, the group established criteria that focused agreement on which overlapping dealers would be eliminated and which should be kept, and what other adjustments, if any, should be made.

Despite the fact that the strategies of each of the two companies historically had been so different, agreeing on 14 criteria dramatically facilitated the entire process so that they were able to reach basic consensus on an action plan for North America, the United Kingdom, the Nordic countries, Germany, Italy, France, and Portugal in only one intensive day. They turned these over to a Business Expansion and Dealer Strategy task force for troubleshooting, who would then report their findings.

The group members also addressed the issue of product line expansion within the context of the tentative decisions already reached, and did so in light of their short-term versus long-term goals. Specifically, they asked, "What new product expansion [*not* improvements] criteria should we use to evaluate our offerings?" On their first cut of criteria, there were a total of 28! Next, they agreed on a set of priorities (Step 4), including the following:

> Major new product expansion projects absolutely must, without fail:
> a. Meet minimum profitability (8 percent Return On Assets) over the life of the product (cycle average).
> b. Achieve minimum revenue of $20 million during the first two years and $38 million by the end of the third year.
> c. Retain the company names and colors.
> d. Avoid any action whatsoever that adversely impacts customer satisfaction for existing or proposed products.

They also identified and valued 23 Desirable Objectives, 8 of which were:

- Maximize profitability and return. [10]
- Maximize revenues. [10]
- Maximize opportunity to use present distribution system. [9]
- Minimize dilution of core business. [9]

- Maximize ability to use present expertise. [7]
- Minimize added investment and fixed cost. [4]
- Achieve and support innovative and creative environment. [3]
- Support and capitalize on our worldwide presence. [2]

Once they had agreed on the prioritized criteria, the managers were able to perform a rigorous evaluation (Steps 5 and 6) of new product and service expansion activities of both companies worldwide. Their tentative decision, subject to further validation during the next several weeks (Step 7), was to go full steam ahead with a major new product line of the acquired company and to plan to discontinue over time several of the acquirer's (Darco's) products.

Now that they knew conceptually what their basic market expansion and dealer and product strategies were for North America and major European markets, they were ready to tackle the toughest challenge: organizational structure.

Lamb urged the group to get a good night's sleep and begin the following morning at 7:00 A.M. so everyone would be rested before attempting to address this most difficult and complex issue. He opened the early morning session by reminding everyone of the importance of the session: "We can't leave here until we've agreed on the shape of the organizational structure. Also, we probably cannot continue to have two presidents, two senior vice-presidents for marketing and sales, and so forth. This won't be an easy task, because of the tendency for people to get defensive and frustrated. But as you've gotten to know one another from the difficult tasks we've already accomplished, and from how I've seen you work together, I know that I can count on each and every one of you to give it your best shot to come up with the best structure to accomplish the objectives we've already agreed on. I'll work closely with anyone in this room whose position is eliminated to help you find a suitable career opportunity, whether inside or outside this organization."

The group first focused on a set of ground rules refined in light of the task, such as "Only one speaker at a time will be recognized by the chairman," "No side conversations," and so forth. Then, using Option Analysis, the group members specified and agreed on a set of criteria (Step 3) to be used to both generate and then evaluate possible options. Originally, they listed more than 70 possible organizational criteria. Some of the more important included:

1. Achieve adequate product line orientation.
2. Must assure achievement of business plan volume.
3. Retain essential (to be named) employees.
4. Achieve the fastest possible capability to identify and satisfy customer needs by maintaining close customer contact and awareness at all levels of the organization.
5. Preserve organizational capability to propagate, manufacture, and sell our major product.
6. Achieve minimum of business plan commitment for organizational savings: 1987 ($3M); 1989 ($10M): 1991 ($19M).
7. Avoid more than two positions reporting directly to CEO with profit responsibility and accountability.

Once agreement was reached on all the criteria, the managers identified the Absolute Requirements (2, 3, and 6—Step 4) and then rated the Desirable Objectives. The final list of Desirable Objectives included the following:

- Highest likelihood of achieving profitable sales. [10]
- Maximize worldwide economics of scale to reduce product cost. [10]
- Highest likelihood of achieving a common direction and strategy for the entire organization. [9]
- Achieve lean, flat organization with minimum levels of reporting relationships. [8]

- Achieve delegation of decision making to the lowest possible level commensurate with security. [8]
- Maximize ability to motivate key employees. [8]
- Highest likelihood of achieving open communication, both inside and outside, with a feedback mechanism to ensure employee buy-in. [7]
- Achieve maximum, effective worldwide interaction between product engineering, manufacturing, and purchasing. [7]

To carry out the next step (Step 5), Identify options ("organizational structures" in this case), Lamb initially divided the two companies into opposite ends of the room to generate alternative options. Lamb soon realized that the groups were spending too much energy discussing why certain organizational structures would look good and others wouldn't. At that point, he stopped the action and said, "Listen, you guys better quit figuring out how to lobby for your pet choice—it's a waste of time. Everyone in this room has two choices: Either you help me get through this organizational analysis and we come out with a structure that everybody agrees and buys into, or you can all go home and let me do it! One way or another, by the end of the week we're going to have a new organizational structure."

Following this stern admonition, the managers then divided into two cross-company teams and proceeded to discuss possible structures. When they reconvened, they found they had generated a total of 14 organizational structures. After eliminating structures that looked somewhat redundant with one another, they ended up with 10 distinct possible organizational realignments ranging from functional or product profit centers to combinations of functional/geographical and geographical/marketing profit centers to geographical/product line organizations.

Agreeing that these 10 represented the universe of possibilities they wished to consider, the managers then divided themselves evenly into two teams, counterparts from the previously competitive companies sitting next to each other. The teams then began evaluating the 10 alternative structures (Step 6), with the intention of returning to the planning session with a recommendation. By the end of a long day and a half, both cross-company teams had agreed that seven of the ten structures could be shot down and that one of the remaining three stood tall next to the other two. The group then spent about 45 minutes as a combined team, trying to shoot down—to destroy—what appeared to be the best structural option. When it withstood the barrage of challenges, it was turned over to an Organizational Structure task force to further troubleshoot and flesh it out, then report back on a specified date with its recommendation together with a communication and implementation plan.

Having used the Option Analysis method to determine the best tentative organizational structure, Lamb turned everyone's attention to such other thorny issues as agreeing on a policy statement on direction and strategy, as well as quality, management style, and so forth. Although many of the decisions that resulted were tentative, pending access to necessary data that was missing from the conference, the opportunity to collaboratively discuss and achieve consensus built tremendous goodwill and esprit de corps so that, when they came to tackle the difficult issue of unionization (the acquirer was heavily unionized and the acquired company had no union), the analysis proceeded smoothly and without intense emotions. What had seemed at the outset a highly volatile issue was resolved agreeably by the development of a *Communication and Implementation Plan* that satisfied everyone's interests. (Part III, Risk Analysis, describes the development of Communication and Implementation Plans.)

By the time it had reached the end of the 6-day conference, the group had even addressed the issue of "How should we measure profitability from this point on?" This had been a divisive and difficult subject prior to the conference, since each company had a totally opposite way of measuring profitability and thought it was turning in far superior results compared to the other. In just a 2½ hour session, the conference attendees were able to discuss the issue and found a resolution that everyone found appropriate and satisfying. It required some refinements of the profitability measurements each company was used to applying, but it made far more sense now that they were one entity and a truly major worldwide player.

Interestingly, senior management of the combined companies used the seven-step Option Analysis method to decide that it made most economic sense to centralize headquarters. (When he had first walked through Kenderson's old and somewhat musty offices, Lamb had felt a surge of excitement. He soaked in Kenderson's laid-back, almost sleepy atmosphere which contrasted so greatly with Darco's hustle and bustle, fast-paced urban headquarters environment. What an opportunity to revitalize Kenderson had been his initial reaction, despite its charm. Fortunately, he had postponed any decision until after the conference, and realized he must be careful in dealing with this matter so as to capitalize on the atmosphere, which, if preserved, was so motivating and congenial for many Kenderson managers.)

The more he thought about it, the more convinced Lamb became that, instead of the acquired firm's moving to the new parent company's location, Darco should move from their metropolitan headquarters to Kenderson's semi-rural headquarters. This decision was taken.

Although the move certainly represented culture shock to Darco's employees, so carefully was the decision thought through and troubleshot (through Risk Analysis—see Part III) that only several managers chose to seek other employment. Even those who initially vehemently protested the move came around to the realization that it was in their company's best interest. Many even decided that the move would better satisfy their own personal and family objectives as they reviewed the Option Analysis objectives and the data from the community so different from their own metropolitan one.

The last major element of the conference was devoted to developing individual communication plans and then integrating them into a cohesive implementation program. This was critical because of the amount of communication that would be necessary to explain to all stakeholders of the two companies, even though the ink wasn't dry on the existing legal paperwork, and closings in various parts of the world would not occur for weeks or even months. This phase of the plan further solidified the team under one banner. There was even agreement to incorporate both company names into the new entity, "The Darco–Kenderson Group."

At the end of the conference, the 16 managers left exhausted but enthusiastic, and eminently satisfied with what they had accomplished. Even those who recognized they would not keep the same position they had when they entered the room at the beginning of the week, or whose fiefdom had been shrunk, were nonetheless excited at the prospect of what they now could accomplish as a combined company with powerful, synergistic resources and capabilities rather than two distinct organizational units.

Following are some points to be learned from the analysis in this chapter:

1. Seven out of ten acquisitions fail to meet the financial objectives and expectations of the buying company, and two out of three are outright failures. The primary reason for this discouraging statistic is that the acquiring firm often lacks a rational decision-making process to determine whether the acquisition represents the best way to grow, and to create an effective postmerger process that will lead to a smooth transition. In this chapter,

the identification of the strong cultural contrasts allowed the acquiring company to deal intelligently with the human and organizational dynamics of the situation, and avert disaster.

2. The president or chairperson of a meeting and all involved should recognize that the process is not a democratic process, but rather a highly collaborative one in which those who have the best experience and knowledge are the ones to be listened to most carefully. This is not to say that sometimes people who are "outside the forest" cannot provide valuable insights about the "trees." Invariably, though, it makes more sense to get relevant inputs and then, instead of everyone having an equal vote, asking the group to offer their assessments of the criteria and their evaluations of the options in terms of how well they score against the Desirable Objectives, listening and paying heed to those whose judgment you consider the best grounded.

3. In this instance, the president split a team that had begun working together. This proved to be counterproductive, because it encouraged people to revert to their habitual ways of thinking and put on their "experiential blinders."

4. Although not reflected in the preceding discussion, the group used frequent "process checks" to help focus everyone on "How well are we doing?" in terms of the Option Analysis process and in their interaction with one another.

5. Positive strokes from the president at several key points were very helpful in giving the group a sense of accomplishment when morale sagged. At some points, positive feedback served as a catalyst for completing the analysis.

6. When there is any major change that will affect others

outside the group doing the analysis, a good detailed and realistic Communication and Implementation Plan is essential. In this instance, several hours were spent on specifying and calendarizing the program in terms of (a) *what* was to happen, (b) *when* it was to be initiated, (c) by *when* the goals were to be accomplished, (d) *who* was accountable, and (e) *what* key resources were needed for each major action item.

How was the Option Analysis process evaluated by senior management of the two former competitors? What was its value added? The written evaluations to the question "In what ways, if any, do you feel the Option Analysis sessions we had *exceeded* your expectations in terms of achieving the mission and principal objectives?" included:

"Covered the very difficult subjects of Direction and Strategy, and eventually Organization Structure, very well and very thoroughly."

"Direction and Strategy actually were agreed upon!"

"Exceeded accomplishments in terms of: Mission, Policy, Organization; and *Great* rapport."

"We reached concensus on the most important strategic issues—that was much more specific than I expected!"

"Effectively handled some tough and complex issues while maintaining very positive relationships—we also got more buy-in on what the priorities were and what the mission and strategy should be."

"Communication between the two management groups was excellent. I'm sure we understand each other's culture much more than we did at the beginning of the week. We addressed a number of very important critical issues and resolved many of them. We exceeded my expectations."

"We covered a tremendous amount of material and successfully completed a major portion of the agenda. I was especially pleased with the work done on the Organization and the way the two groups worked together."

Small wonder that this acquisition and resultant merger were successful—when the acquirer sold off its holding 3 years later, it realized a 32 percent return on its investment!

CHAPTER SIX

Option Analysis
in Action—3:
Further Up
the Organization

When Michael Demis was "parachuted" in as the new chief financial and administrative officer of Exeter Group, a manufacturer of trucks and recreational vans, he quickly discovered that one of his first major challenges would be to turn around the poor earnings performance of the organization's Credit Company. With more than $1 billion in wholesale segments, as well as retail segment investments exceeding $2 billion, the Company wasn't performing up to its potential. Since the founding of the Group, the Credit Company had played a supporting and subservient role to the three Strategic Business Units (SBUs), essentially to help them sell more trucks and vans. The Company shared responsibility for managing the wholesale loan portfolio, which caused considerable frustration to people in both organizations.

Policies for managing the business were either not clear-cut, not current, or simply not adhered to consistently. Attention was needed in such areas as management of aged receivables, reduction of dealer float, reduction of dealer abuse of certain programs, continued relationships with dealers that had inadequate or marginal performance, and development of early warning systems to protect against fraud.

Group executives had met and agreed that management in this important area would be improved by centralizing the activity within one specific area of responsibility. This was discussed at great length in terms of pros and cons. The issues were as follows:

Divisional. The Credit Company would restructure its operation according to a pure retail strategy. All resources supporting the wholesale portfolio would be either eliminated or repositioned within the SBUs. Headcount would be reduced by as many as 30 people and consolidation of 12 Sales Finance Office networks considered further. The Credit Company headcount reduction, however, would be more than offset because of the need to set up management of the inventory in two separate business units.

Although the business unit credit function would be well integrated and responsive to unit needs, care would have to be exercised not to subordinate important credit controls to sales objectives. Immediate reorganization along these lines would be difficult and time-consuming, and extreme caution would have to be exercised to preserve credit quality. Also, once completed, it would be difficult to move the wholesale function back to the Credit Company.

Functional. The Credit Company would assume responsibility for the SBU credit functions. It would provide complete inventory and credit services to the business units. Headcount totaling 21 people would transfer directly to the Credit Company with no net gain to the Group on a consolidated basis. Clearly, communication and responsiveness by the Credit Company to SBU needs would have to improve; at best, they might not reach levels resulting from organizational structuring along divisional lines.

The Credit Company, however, hopefully would provide cost-effective and consistent service to the Group system, as well as ensuring that independent controls were maintained. Organization along these lines would necessitate a broader Credit Company strategic focus and, in the following year, a resource allocation to the wholesale business at the expense of the retail business. In the longer run, retail business would probably be enhanced because of the closer ongoing contact with the Credit Company's major channel of distribution, the Dealer network. This strategy would provide organizational flexibility downstream, since shifting wholesale credit to a divisional structure could be implemented if the Credit Company maintained some separation in the wholesale and retail businesses going forward.

The organization along divisional lines would have a significant impact on the Credit Company's financial performance. In terms of the next fiscal year's budget, pretax income of $76.4 million (net income of $58.5 million) would be reduced by $50.9 million to $25.5 million. This profitability, essentially generated internally, would shift over to the SBUs. On the incremental expense side, headcount increases in the SBUs would have to be weighed in the context of headcount reductions and possible office consolidations at the Credit Company. Organization along functional lines would simply involve shifting salary and related overhead of 21 people from the SBUs to the Credit Company.

The best strategy would optimize the mix of credit quality, customer responsiveness, and flexibility to maximize the profit potential for the Group's business units in the future. Therefore, it was imperative that a timely decision be made, so that the Credit Company could carefully define its future mission in the second quarter of the following year and begin to implement its strategy for the 1990s.

In addition to the foregoing strategic issue, there were also very real here-and-now Responsibility/Authority/Accountability issues, specifically three that had to be resolved before Demis could develop an action plan: Who should make the decision about whether to finance a dealer's inventory? Should the Credit Corporation be allowed to finance a dealer's competing floor plan inventory? Who's responsible for auditing Dealer inventory, the Finance Credit Officer or the Finance SBU marketing manager?

* * *

Within hours after "touching down" at his new home base, Demis noticed that a major concern was rivalry between the Credit Company and the SBUs, characterized by a destructive "we/they" mental set. The SBUs also viewed the Credit Company as both a necessary evil and a second-class citizen. Further digging through confidential interviews and a survey revealed that the underlying question among Credit Company managers was whether the Company should be responsible for financing Dealer inventory (Wholesale) or should focus entirely on End User financing (Retail). Wholesale had been a sacred cow within the Credit organization for many years and represented a substantial (albeit unprofitable) piece of Credit's Book of Business.

Demis, who had used Option Analysis at his previous company, decided that this was the issue to be resolved, and that it should best be discussed at an off-site team-building and Option Analysis work conference.

At the conference, which was held 2 weeks later, a team of 15 Home Office, Regional Office, and Field Credit managers learned how to use Option Analysis, and they began immediately tackling the problems at hand. Normally, they would have simply "smoked out the issues" (Step 1) and then developed a Mission Statement for the Credit Company. But one of the senior managers, who had recently participated in a 2-day retreat with his former employer, complained that "a dozen other guys and I wasted two days in the woods communing with squirrels. It was nice, but totally worthless." In deference to this manager's experience, Demis suggested that the group first agree on the criteria (Step 3) for determining an appropriate Credit Company Mission Statement. This specification, to be met by whatever Mission Statement they approved, included:

105

1. One sentence, 25 words or less.
2. Customer-satisfaction focus.
3. Profitability focus.
4. Credibility.
5. Motivation.
6. Quality-driven.

By first agreeing on the criteria, the group was able to save considerable time that otherwise would have been frittered away in arguing about the pros and cons of different possible statements. Within a half-hour, everyone agreed on the Mission Statement.

> To ensure customer satisfaction by delivering quality financial products and services while achieving an acceptable return.

The group then fleshed out each word of that statement, defining the measures of performance so that all employees would understand specifically what every single element in the general statement meant, in order that they view this as the reasonable and necessary raison d'être of the company.

Next, they applied Step 2 for determining how the credit function for the Group's Wholesale business should be managed in order to acheive an optimal balance between the Sales' objectives of achieving solid growth and Credit's objectives of protecting company assets and limiting company exposure to loss.

They agreed on criteria (Step 3), including:

1. What should be achieved:
   a. Create an independent credit function.
   b. Implement a rational organization of wholesale credit to achieve a proper balance of responsibility, authority, and accountability.
   c. Create a structure that is reasonably flexible in view of changing organizational characteristics and requirements.

2. What should be preserved:
   a. Well-managed wholesale portfolio of high credit standards.
   b. Responsiveness to dealers.
3. What should be avoided:
   a. Deterioration of portfolio credit quality.
   b. Deterioration of responsiveness to dealers.
   c. Excessive "headcount" anywhere in the credit organization.
   d. Organizational chaos.

The management group (which was now really functioning as one team) then prioritized the total list of criteria, agreeing first on those measurable objectives that *had* to be achieved (i.e., Absolute Requirements) in order to deliver what was necessary and "ratioing" the Desirable Objectives accordingly.

In evaluating the two basic options with several variations of each, the team discovered that the Wholesale part of the business didn't belong within Credit Company, given the agreed-on Absolute Requirements and Desirable Objectives. Rather, Wholesale should more effectively be housed in the three SBUs, giving them full accountability and authority for inventory and other Wholesale issues.

Because the managers had attacked the issue with a task (rather than a personality) focus and followed an agreed-on road map to Option Analysis to arrive at the best decision, they were able to put aside parochial thinking and "hobby horses" to achieve consensus. The final decision reflected commitment from everyone involved, despite the fact that many in the group had begun the analysis believing that the Credit Company should not relinquish this significant area of responsibility—and profitability.

On the last day of the conference, the team recognized that it needed to determine what should be communicated by whom, to whom, by when, and how. Again, instead of charging right into the issue to discuss the pros and cons, they first agreed on a prioritized list of 22 criteria, including the following:

Very High in Importance
- Achieve credibility with everyone to whom we communicate.
- Preserve continuity of the day-to-day operations of the business.

High in Importance
- Achieve recipient understanding of the reasons for and benefits of our decision to divest the Wholesale side of our business and transfer it to the Product SBUs.
- Achieve highest likelihood of the CEO's and the SBUs' accepting this.
- Achieve their sense that Credit Company still has a definite and appropriate future direction.
- Achieve their perception of this decision and its execution as having been well conceived and planned.

Also Important
- Achieve their understanding of who was involved in the decision.
- Achieve their understanding that this is in fact a transition period.
- Achieve employee understanding of and motivation for the change.
- Achieve their feeling of being part of the team even though they weren't involved in reaching the decision.
- Preserve the loyalty and dedication of our workforce.
- Preserve the positive attitude of our Dealers.
- Avoid the loss of good employees.
- Avoid in any way alienating the three Strategic Business Units.

It was decided that the following key points to be communicated best met the criteria, and that they should be circulated on a limited basis to those who needed to know the current state of the decision-making process.

1. The decision has been reached that there is going to be an orderly transfer of Wholesale Inventory Accounting from the Credit Company to the Strategic Business Units.
2. In the short term, we will hold onto the Wholesale function while transitioning in a phased manner to a completely Retail organization.
3. We need to continue to do as good a job as we have, or even better, at our responsibilities as the Wholesale transfer proceeds.
4. We've already identified a new Mission Statement along with three major Key Result Areas of our Retail business in which we can really excel (i.e., customer satisfaction, organizational structure, and profitability).
5. We have agreed on objectives in each of these Areas and specific strategies to accomplish them. These will be shared with you within the next several weeks.
6. We also have begun planning for training programs and the development of a business plan, and are already committing to dates to progress toward and accomplish all of this.
7. Transition teams are being formed to shed the Wholesale function.
8. We feel enthusiastic focusing strictly on the Retail business after the transition!
9. The Field Offices are now involved in this process and will continue to be involved. It's going to be a process developed jointly with broad participation across the Credit Company and the SBUs.

(In Chapter 10 in the Risk Analysis section, you'll read about the Troubleshooting process that the group used. For now, look at the key Organizational Structure issue they tackled next.)

Demis expanded a second conference to include 24 managers from the Credit Company. This was the conference, as several described it somewhat apprehensively, where the "rubber will meet the road"; here, the group would have to address difficult organizational issues, with all the attendant job and career implications. Since the decision had already been made to transfer the Wholesale function to the three Strategic Business Units, the issue would be, "How can we best implement this Strategy?"

To answer this complex question, criteria setting again proved invaluable (Step 3). Following are some of the key criteria the participants developed:

The best implementation plan *absolutely must, without fail:*
a. Be fully operational no later than December 31.
b. Achieve the Operating budget for the next fiscal year.
Among Desirable Objectives:
c. Achieve 5-year profitability goals. [10]
   1. Retail collection performance. [5]
   2. Expense budgets. [2]
   3. Measurability of P&L. [2]
   4. Adjustment criteria. [1]
d. Achieve a strong Win/Win customer focus. [10]
   1. Quick response time for one-on-one support in interaction with Dealers. [5]
   2. Strong bond among the three operating units. [1]
   3. Quick response time to Dealers and Stores on approvals. [3]
   4. Prompt, accurate competitive intelligence. [1]
e. Achieve clear-cut delegation of Responsibility/Authority/Accountability and effective communication. [8]
   1. Less management, more leadership. [5]
   2. Maximum motivation/utilization of people. [3]
f. Fully operational ASAP. [6]
g. Capitalize on current available technology. (Manage-

ment Information Systems, new Retail note-processing system, and other new technology.) [4]

(Note that if a Desirable Objective was stated in rather broad terms and included several component pieces—and was also subject to misinterpretation—the overall value of that objective was subdivided among those pieces in ratio to one another. This assures consensus regarding the relative importance of these. It also helps in the evaluation of options by indicating what more-precise information has to be gathered and addressed about each, while facilitating assessment of how well each option scores against each component.)

After prioritizing these criteria, the team researched ways in which other competitors were structured. Demis then guided the managers as they generated and evaluated nine options, including the present organizational structure. When all was said and done, a clear "winner" did evolve. This entailed a reduction of 121 Field personnel, many of whom were transferred to the Strategic Business Units, where they focused on the Wholesale business. This left the Credit Division with 207 full-time positions instead of the original 328.

According to Demis, "After this Option Analysis process, people understood what had been agreed to and why it had been agreed to. Even if it wasn't the position they had wanted, they fell in behind it. Without this kind of process, we wouldn't have gotten that kind of buy-in."

Six months after the project, the Credit Company was a long way down the road toward implementing the strategies, and was even exceeding its financial objectives. As just one example, in several months it had won an additional $10 million in sales of Retail line business from competitors. One year later, the Credit Company had delivered $50 million worth of additional sales, carved from competitors!

The success of this program can be measured in a number of additional ways, according to Demis:

- "The Credit Company is the only company of the four SBUs currently doing well in the Corporation."
- "The new strategy of going after credit contracts for non-SBU products pulled in $90 million the second year!"
- "The amazing thing to me is that this was with an initial cast of players I inherited who were not strong managers. Having a process really helped get us back into action and weed out 'farm hands' from 'keepers.'"
- "Although some of the feedback was frustrating and painful, it was well worth it. The benefit of the feedback was that everybody saw the situation in the same way, and the Option Analysis conference resulted in people feeling the ideas were theirs. We achieved consensus with everyone agreeing and 'falling in behind' the decisions reached, even though I had already made up my mind beforehand about some of them."
- "Another new strategy gives Dealers credit toward the purchase of equipment if they exceed their objective. Dealers so far this year have earned $1.2 million in this new program, and this at a time when the market is terrible and everybody in the industry is suffering, typically downsizing their organizations by 20 to 30 percent!"
- "Another benefit was the Decision and Risk Analysis techniques which we wouldn't have done otherwise. It forced people who never have thought strategically in their entire life to do so."

This application of Option Analysis shows how effective it can be when used as a *diagnostic* and *integrative* management tool—diagnostic in the sense of analyzing a very complex, fixed-outcome problem that generates a good deal of emotion and polarized opinions, and integrative in terms of the process itself, which melds groups of managers with differing perspectives and judgments.

Demis made excellent use of the process, beginning with

his recognition that a major issue was the "we/they" rivalry between the Credit Company and the SBUs. He understood that the key to achieving a Common Vision is letting the players experience frustration as they weigh the pros and cons of a major complex decision, finding that there is anything but unanimity of agreement.

Demis also hired a professional third party to interview key managers of the three SBUs and the Credit Company in order to get buy-in from *all* parties about what the key issues seemed to be *before* proceeding ahead to engage just the Credit Company in the Option Analysis of the Wholesale and Inventory issues. He also made certain that there was agreement first on the criteria and then on their priorities *before* allowing any discussion of the Options—and then ensured full understanding of what each option meant before evaluating it against the criteria.

Of great importance was the investment of several hours in defining criteria for *the best* Communication and Implementation Plan. (See Part III, Risk Analysis.) Prioritizing the criteria, rather than shortcutting the process, once again ensured everyone's buy-in and commitment to what had to be achieved, preserved, and avoided. The team then evolved a plan out of the criteria that would indeed be achievable.

This major application of Option Analysis, which proved so successful in terms of capturing a significant market share from the competition, coupled with Demis's excellent leadership in other areas, motivated Exeter Group's CEO to appoint Demis as head of the largest of the three SBUs, where he continues to use the process with his management group in order to cope with very difficult market conditions.

* * *

Now consider another example that shows how this decision-making process can be applied to "Rightsizing" an organization. Norman Kample, a division vice-president and general manager of a large steel manufacturer, faced making a complex and ultimately unpleasant decision. Although his division was still making a good profit, the market for its product was shrinking fast. In addition, the Canadian parent corporation continued to use the division as its major "cash cow," draining its income to fund other, more-promising divisions. And because of dwindling demand for the division's major product line, the parent company withdrew all capital investment support, except for what the division could generate itself after meeting the stringent profit and cash flow requirements of the parent. The division thus found itself in a double bind: Management was required to produce profits without being given the resources to expand the business. This forced a massive cost reduction. So Kample was handed the task of "determining the best way(s) to meet stringent corporate financial objectives for the next three years."

Rather than "cut headcount" and make other decisions unilaterally, use just one or two confidants, or have a management consultant "whisper in his ear what he should do," Kample decided to conduct an Option Analysis session, pulling his plant managers and senior staff together so that they could collaboratively address the issues at hand. After gathering data on what the key issues were as perceived by managers, key customers, selected vendors, and several other influential constituencies, Kample convened the group at a rustic offsite location 120 miles north of Toronto. The group, operating under a common vision and understanding of the issues, established and prioritized the Criteria (Steps 3 and 4), then developed possible strategic options.

One possible strategy was to shut down one or more of the four manufacturing plants, thereby dramatically reducing costs. No one in the group favored this idea because there were so many potential adverse consequences, including the probability that the involved provincial governments would take retaliatory action since they were aggressively trying to attract industry to the two economically depressed areas of Canada in which all the plants happened to be located.

Such factors strongly motivated the search for other options. Suggestions included:

- Increase international sales in several specific ways.
- Lobby municipal governments for changes in product specifications to permit use of more products (as well as ones with different specifications).
- Develop particular new products.
- Sell off equipment and raw materials.
- Distribute specific related products for other companies.

The group recognized that it lacked certain information, but it still made a series of tentative judgments and then recessed for four days to gather what information was necessary to continue with and finalize their analysis. At the second meeting, they slightly refined the criteria in terms of their up-to-date knowledge of the situation, and then—through their painstaking evaluation of the options against the criteria—they found that their original hypothesis that it would be necessary to "shut down at least one plant" was not necessary. What they found was that they were able to come up with a combination of 14 different strategies to meet the corporate financial objectives for the next 3 years. Some of the strategies entailed the sale of certain raw materials and equipment, closing off certain areas of two plants to save electricity and heat, reducing payroll by 10 percent across several plants, entering into an agreement to distribute certain related but noncompetitive products for other manufacturers, granting price concessions to customers for immediate bulk purchases of certain products and services, and wringing price concessions from several vendors.

Everyone left the conference with a commitment to explain the process and the decisions to their employees, union representatives, customers and vendors, provincial governments, and other key constituencies. The process had short-cir-cuited any grumbler who might have loudly announced, "I wasn't part of that decision, and I don't care what happens." And it had left everyone his or her personal management dignity and self-worth.

Because the union representatives, government officials, and others found the explanation reasonable for the strategies selected, as well as those rejected, and because the group had painstakenly taken into account the human aspects and impact of their decisions, all accepted what they were told and didn't take an adversarial position.

* * *

As this second example shows, there are times when you may want to involve others right at the start of the process. Initially, you may not have a broad enough information base to make a sound decision. And you may realize that in order to get everyone's cooperation, they will have to be part of the decision. Or you may recognize that if the decision is to be implemented properly, the team must work with you during the whole analysis process. Finally, you've undoubtedly recognized that participation in the process can be powerfully persuasive in winning the approval of others, be it your boss, a prospect or customer, close associates, your spouse and children, and so forth. Involving others in your decision is probably one of the most helpful things you can do; by letting others be a part of your decision-making process, they can provide an added level of information, experience, perspective, and judgment. This is also the best way to create "buy-in" to a decision as well as to ensure that communications, implementation, and follow-through for that decision will be carried out to the best of your managers' abilities.

Following are some guidelines to consider when choosing whether to involve people in your decision. You should involve others in your decision when:

1. Their input could significantly increase the quality of and confidence in the decision.
2. Their acceptance is important to the successful communication or implementation of the decision.
3. Failure to include them would have serious effects on future relationships.
4. Their acceptance of the decision is not an issue and yet you truly believe (as do knowledgeable others) that you do not have the necessary knowledge and information to make the best decision.
5. Someone has really already made the decision and the purpose in involving others is to see if they would come to the same or similar conclusion. Don't, however, try to manipulate them into believing that they played a role in making the decision; you might be surprised how transparent this is, how readily people "see through" this ruse—or believe that this indeed is the case!

There are times when both the quality of the decision and its acceptance by others are equally important. At such times, you may have to evaluate the "trade-offs" involved in choosing one option over the other, possibly sacrificing an "ideal" decision for one that is almost as good but will have better "buy-in" and higher probability of effective execution.

Not all people want to participate in decision making, and attempts to involve them can be acutely frustrating. Beyond those who may be lazy, or simply do not want to take responsibility, what may be some factors?

First, some people simply do not feel adequate to the task; they honestly do not see how they can make a meaningful contribution to a decision. They may feel, incorrectly, that what they could offer "couldn't possibly be of value." Or they may consider themselves just "not smart enough" to help make an important decision. Participation for them for whatever reason could be anxiety-producing and even painful.

Another possible source of reluctance to become involved in making a decision is fear of disagreement or criticism. The possibility of saying something about which others may not approve can make people feel very uncomfortable and reluctant to risk being criticized (particularly if the president or other presiding person tends to hold a grudge against those who disagree with his or her opinion).

In general, however, presidents and senior managers who opt to use this Option Analysis process are not the type of people to hold grudges against those who disagree with them. In fact, it is a way to learn from and gain respect for opposing views. New CEOs especially appreciate the Option Analysis process because, by involving new senior management, it allows the CEO direct access to their thinking process while instructing them to input to the analysis what they know or believe. In other words, people's input to this type of process is a reflection of how their minds operate and a clue to how "close to the vest" they may play things. It will also give you a clue as to how well others communicate. For example, some people are very logically oriented, whereas others are more emotional, and some share information more readily than others.

One CEO of a leading service organization used Option Analysis with his senior management first to develop a new organizational structure for the company and then to appoint people to new positions. This new organizational structure had eliminated some of the positions of those who reported directly to him, who were sitting around the table (and created a few new ones, as well). All of the participants had equal access and input to the decisions reached, and all agreed to do away with the positions and add new ones.

The CEO and the management group developed the Mission or Charters of each of the newly created positions and also specified them for the existing positions, a total of the 16 senior positions in the company. This helped in both specifying and focusing on the priorities so that all could agree on the necessary criteria for each position. Each senior position was then open for anyone in the senior team to designate himself or herself and one or two others as alternative candidates to be evaluated against the suggested position.

As each position was addressed, the CEO excused anyone present who was to be considered for it; the group then evaluated those individuals against other candidates. The CEO and the senior vice-president of human resources were the only two who possessed a record of each candidate, including performance and promotability appraisals, and so forth. The CEO and the remainder of his senior team performed each evaluation, drawing on their knowledge, perceptions, and the information possessed by the CEO and the human resources executive. The process went extremely well. All in all, everyone was satisfied with the positions on which the group agreed, including where each individual ended, even though there were four people who accepted major position changes.

After a year, only one of the original nine people who participated in the evaluation left—and that was for a promotion in the parent company!

Again, remember that the quality of analysis has a lot to do with the leadership and integrity of the process and commitment by the management team to what's best for the whole organization, even if it means there may be some personal disappointments.

But as a leader, how can you judge how much confidence you should have in a decision? Following are eight criteria for testing the validity of a decision; you may want to add more of your own:

1. A "quality" decision instills confidence.
2. You have a sufficient amount of accurate data or information on which to base your decision. You may have asked, "What exactly do I need to know in order to make this decision, and how would I go about getting

this information?" Unless you've done a thorough job at this, you may feel apprehensive about your decision.

3. The decision was clearly necessary and directed to the "real" issues.

4. The decision appears to achieve the basic premise or purpose for making that decision and fulfills your criteria better than any other alternative.

5. The decision coincides with your values, beliefs, and norms. It "feels good"; it's appropriate to the situation, and makes you feel "good" about yourself.

6. It is a well-balanced decision (i.e., you achieve your criteria without too great a risk to available resources and don't foresee any serious, probable, additional problems created by the decision).

7. You can defend it logically and support it objectively.

8. It was developed with the help of people who will be implementing the decision or, if not, you are confident that those who implement the decision will understand and "buy into" it and also will be depending on its success.

At the same time, you've probably found that so many decisions seem good in one's mind or look good on paper, but don't work! Execution of decisions is a critical factor, which is why Step 7 of the Decision Process, Troubleshooting, is so important.

Finally, the best decision is a balanced decision—one that logically best achieves the satisfaction of your criteria, including your values and feelings, and that reduces your risks to an acceptable level. (This aspect is discussed in the third part of this book, Risk Analysis.)

CHAPTER SEVEN

Option Analysis
in Action—4:
Wiring the Team
Together

THE COMPANY WITH A
THOUSAND FIEFDOMS

The new president of the Latin American Region (LAR), Jean Pierre, inherited a tough situation: a company operating in 21 Latin American countries with 26 district offices, 128 smaller offices, and 5 sales agents. Although the Profit Plan called for $170 million before taxes, the latest forecast was for only $150 million. Several members of the management group told the president that there was a "good possibility LAR would do somewhat better than this," but volume growth was projected at only 3 percent per year. Market strategies for most of the major countries were vague, as were Action Plans for implementing the plans. Worse, field reports indicated increasing competition.

Given his strong marketing background, the competitive issue particularly caught Jean Pierre's attention. He concluded that Mitsubishi, Fuji, Schindler, and Westinghouse were making significant inroads into his business in various countries. Consequently, by the end of his second week on the job, Jean Pierre insisted on immediately receiving two reports from each country manager: one on product quality and the other on competition. After poring over the reports for an entire weekend with several of his staff, he recognized that product quality and cost seemed to be a major competitive weakness. How could he tackle these issues in a compressed time period while establishing his leadership and uniting each country toward a common mission?

Jean Pierre determined that the best approach would be to pull together all the country managers. He recognized, however, that the problems facing Panama, Uruguay, and Puerto Rico might be very different from those facing Argentina, Brazil, and Venezuela. To determine the differences, he first sought input from each of the countries. When he received the feedback from interviews conducted with managers as well as with major customers and suppliers in Argentina, Brazil, Colombia, Costa Rica, Mexico, Panama, Peru, Puerto Rico, Uruguay, and Venezuela and from Florida headquarters, there was both good and bad news. Although the image of LAR received twice as many positive responses as negative—with the major strengths being its name and reputation, products, market position, and human resources—the biggest negative was the deterioration of the Region's image and the fact that there did not appear to be a single outstanding strength, capability, or distinctive resource compared with a year ago!

Indeed, as Jean Pierre suspected, 50 percent of his own people throughout Latin America mentioned marketing deficiencies as a problem, with almost a third citing poor product quality, especially in their number 1 market—Brazil. This was especially serious since Brazil's long-term role was to become the primary source of product for all of Latin America and the secondary source of product worldwide. Yet, its product quality, delivery service, and sales were only marginal at best, and its relationships with the other countries poor.

One-third of the respondents also criticized the lack of business strategy and planning, given the Region's short-term perspective, lack of teamwork, poor communications, middle-management deficiencies, and excessive historical focus on short-term financials.

As you can well imagine, perceptions about potential changes in the business environment differed country by country, with Brazil, Mexico, Venezuela, and Argentina projected to be the growth areas and focus of competitive thrust.

Mitsubishi was seen as the toughest competitor at the high end of the business, and Schindler at both the low and high ends not only in terms of introducing new technology, product quality and reliability, and meeting schedules, but also in terms of communicating the quality of its product to customers and its unrivaled customer service.

Surprisingly, two-thirds of those interviewed mentioned that LAR mistakenly thought that the plan must be met at all costs. This in turn made the organization too short-term profit-oriented. Close to one-third of the respondents also reported a need to clarify the roles and authority of headquarters regarding the operating companies, and 60 percent criticized the ways decisions were made; the leading concern in this area was that decisions were mandated without input from people who really knew the country and its market. Finally, two-thirds also cited problems between Latin American headquarters and the operating companies.

The most pressing issues included:

1. Jean Pierre's boss had made a commitment to the board of directors that Brazil would be used as a "world supplier." This entailed implementing an acquisition in that country. Preliminary feedback indicated that other country managers didn't want to work with Brazil.

2. With regard to LAR's image and reputation, there was an acute credibility problem in two of the countries in which the company had closed factories. Many customers didn't believe that the company would stay in Brazil or service them adequately.

   Jean Pierre would need to demonstrate better linkage with customers and with the countries involved so that the market would believe that there was indeed continuity, stability, responsibility, and—most important—quality. In short, professionalism needed to be ensured, from manufacturing to sales, support, and administration.

3. There was a suggestion on the part of some of the country managers and home office staff that Jean Pierre was somewhat of a "crisis manager" since he had asked for so much information so rapidly, and so early in his tenure.

4. The operating companies were accustomed to being talked *at,* not *with.* Regional conferences were largely "dog and pony shows" and didn't deal with real issues.

5. The companies hesitated to say anything negative to the home office staff because, too often, their comments would be taken out of context or blown out of proportion.

6. Home office staff dictated policy changes without understanding or considering their impact on the real issues in various countries.

7. Headquarters staff demonstrated the attitude that they had to find something wrong. So instead of trying to help companies, they just focused on what was *not* good.

8. From a marketing perspective, questions remained, such as: Is the market really there? Are projections realistic? Do we have sufficient resources to meet these projections? Can we get the business at our protected margins? Product coverage in some countries is partic-

ularly weak—why aren't materials written in the language of the particular country? New products should be introduced properly with sales literature, technical training, and so forth.

9. The home office was particularly criticized for its excessive reporting requirements—"avalanches of paper," as one manager put it.

10. There was also a real concern with specifying the authority of the LAR staff in terms of country managers and defining various functional responsibilities both in the home office and within operating companies.

11. Finally, there was a definite need for a strategy and plan in order to provide the necessary ability to attract and motivate, reward, and retain more-qualified people.

In addition to the foregoing, the single most important action or result that Jean Pierre had to achieve was to foster a common vision and sense of teamwork. Two-thirds of the managers from within the various countries and headquarters agreed that this was the number 1 issue, with 50 percent urging that further investments be made to modernize operations, especially in Brazil.

Armed with this information, Jean Pierre decided it would be helpful to share the entire feedback report word-for-word with the country managers and their deputies. The text of his memo follows:

> We can look back on the last few years in LAR with pride. You were able to overcome many difficult obstacles and achieve ever increasing higher goals. To help ensure our continued long-term success, it now seems timely that our management group take stock of where we are today as an organization, where we want to be in the future, what are the obstacles in our way, and how we can best get there.
>
> At the same time, I am anxious to develop a more open climate and dialogue among the management group in order to

achieve greater unity of purpose, cohesion, and management effectiveness. Accordingly, this letter confirms my request that you reserve October 13-17 for a General Managers' meeting to be held in Fort Myers, Florida.

I've received feedback from the fifty-six interviews with managers, key customers, and suppliers, and wish to share this with all of you so that we can:

1. Agree on what the Priority Issues are that must be resolved to strengthen our market and management effectiveness.
2. Achieve greater unity of purpose and direction.
3. Review the most appropriate direction, goals and objectives, strategies and plans, and program priorities to facilitate resolving our key issues.
4. Make necessary decisions and plans, then follow through to ensure that our plans are implemented effectively.

To address and resolve these issues, Jean Pierre announced that a general managers' meeting representing each country would then be held 1 month later, the goal of which was to:

- Agree on the priority issues for strengthening our market and managing effectiveness.
- Achieve greater unity of purpose and direction.
- Review the most-appropriate options.
- Select courses of action.

In preparing for the conference, Jean Pierre realized that his predecessor's "hub and spoke" basis for conveying information and making decisions would not work any more. The authoritarian management style of his predecessor had simply created resentment and was counterproductive.

To keep the conference on target, he developed the following objectives for himself:

1. Learn to understand the Latin temperament.
2. Foster a danger-free environment so managers can say what they really feel and not hold back for fear of antagonizing me or others.

126

3. Foster teamwork and communication necessary to achieve those strategies.

4. Throttle CYA (cover your ass) and NIH (not invented here) behavior.

5. Broaden the parochial thinking and country self-interest while rewarding attitudes that demonstrate "Let's do what's best for LAR."

6. Demonstrate, whenever possible, that I value consensus rather than unilateral decision making.

7. Improve integration of the managers' efforts.

8. Avoid trying to make "one country" of the Region.

9. Achieve development of a broad, long-range strategy and common vision for the LAR group.

10. Reward teamwork both on an intercompany and a home office country basis.

Given the mix of nationalities and mother tongues in the group (American English, French, Spanish, Portuguese, German, and Dutch), Jean Pierre very carefully carried out a Risk Analysis on what could go wrong. (See Part III for a complete description of the Risk Analysis process.) The following seemed to be among the major potential problems, any one of which could seriously derail productivity of the session:

1. Jean Pierre himself could be called out of the session for a period of time by his boss or some emergency.

2. The president of the Brazil operations, who was used to running his own show, could be uncomfortable with a more consensual process than he had previously experienced, as well as resenting issues that he might feel should be his alone to solve instead of having them discussed in such an open forum.

3. It was clear from the feedback that the country managers and customers felt (rightly or wrongly) that headquarters staff had too much power. As a result, the proceedings might break down into a "we/they" argument.

4. The people could get fatigued.

5. Transfer pricing was a major problem among the countries, especially since Brazil, as the major component supplier, had the reputation of "gouging" the others to the point where they were increasingly seeking other sources of supply.

6. Increasing the focus on strategic and operational issues might be achieved at the expense of the strong financial orientation (viewed as one of the Region's greatest strengths), creating an imbalance.

At the conference, to help loosen up the group and get people to drop their defenses, Jean Pierre divided the 41 managers into three different groups, each in a different room. In each room, the men and women played a business simulation game. The game was tailored to the Region and Jean Pierre's goals. It brought out the following points:

- The region has a lot of muscle that it's not using, because the countries are not working together toward a common goal.
- The managers are more cooperative within their departments, less among the companies, and even less as a Region.
- Pricing policies can be made to be "Win/Win."
- If only the Region's own source of supply provided the quality needed, everyone would benefit. The dollar value would be tremendous.
- The Region has to identify what our objectives are, including how to get the supply source (Brazil) to increase product and service quality. (The supplier might decrease its own profit by increasing quality, but the total profit for LAR would be higher. Also, volume would increase.)
- People in the Region often assume agreements and cooperation when they don't really exist.

- Currently the profit-sharing program is based on local or company profits and not on overall LAR profit. This will have to be changed if Brazil is really going to be used to source product, as planned.

The next day, the group began working on Step 1 of the Option Analysis process, Smoke out the issues. Prior to the meeting, each country manager had been asked to fill out a Root Cause Analysis form that nailed down the *identity*, *location*, and *time* of each particular problem—as well as what, where, and when it was *not* happening, and the relevant distinctions.

This in turn enabled them to rule out a series of possible but not probable causes so that they could indeed identify, in most instances, where the solution could be found (i.e., was it most apt to be an Engineering/Manufacturing, Field, or Inventory type solution?). This saved an enormous amount of time (and argument) that otherwise would have been expended, based on past experience.

After discussing the issues that the individual members had identified on their own, the group smoked out 23 *remaining* issues of concern to the Region. Further discussion revealed one overriding issue:

To determine the best ways to improve, expand, and modernize the business.

This combined issue-purpose statement (Steps 1 and 2) led to the next step, set criteria (Step 3). By the end of the morning session, the group had identified a lengthy list, some entries of which included:

- Achieve profitability.
- Achieve total LAR participation in any program we develop.
- Improve customer relations and contacts.
- Improve business retention.

- Reduce service inventories.
- Reduce callbacks.
- Improve LAR's image with customers and employees.
- Improve technical support.
- Avoid necessary service and repairs.
- Avoid long shutdown time (inconveniencing users).
- Transform competitors' equipment into our equipment. (On reflection, the group realized that this was a possible option and not a criterion.)
- Achieve the maximum standardization possible.
- Avoid adverse impact on the new sales market.
- Reduce vulnerability to competition.
- Avoid damaging the maintenance function.
- Minimize complexity.

Even though the total criteria were extensive, by applying the Absolute Requirement test questions, only two ended up as Absolute Essentials: Whatever we do to expand the modernization of the business, we must, without fail:

1. Achieve a minimum of $10 million incremental sales from modernization and repair.
2. Achieve a minimum of $3 million incremental margin by December 30, annually.

Next, the group evaluated and rated the remaining Desirable Criteria, some of which are listed.

- Achieve modernization as a new, additional way of life. [10]
- Improve business retention. [9]
- Maximize customer satisfaction. [9]
- Minimize $1.5 million SG&A (selling, general, and administrative costs). [9]
- Achieve maximum standardization and rationalization. [8]
- Achieve improved profitability of maintenance contracts after modernization. [6]

- Reduce vulnerability to competition. [2]
- Avoid competing with ourselves. [2]
- Avoid unnecessary service and repairs. [2]

The next step was to determine what options should be considered to improve, expand, and modernize the business. The 41 managers, who by now had melded as one management team, identified an extensive range but managed to organize them into four general categories.

1. Expand and modernize all of the Latin American Region as a whole with headquarters staff support.
2. Expand and modernize each country, but do so with lesser or greater emphasis depending on the particular situation of the country in question.
3. Option 2 plus headquarters staff support.
4. Centralize the expansion and modernization of the small countries, while decentralizing the process for each large country.

For a full day and a half, the managers evaluated the options against the criteria (see Table 7.1), recognizing along the way where they needed further information. The fax and telex machines hummed as the managers requested and received the necessary information from headquarters and the various countries. Finally, they agreed that Option 3 (Expand and modernize each country, but with lesser or greater emphasis depending on the particular situation of the country and with solid headquarters staff support) was the best tentative solution—tentative because there remained several key questions that would have to be further studied to ensure that the data on which they had based certain crucial judgments was solid.

Once the data was confirmed, Jean Pierre assigned a team the task of refining the tentative decision and developing a communication and implementation plan. While this team

Table 7.1 *Modernizing the Business:*
The best way to improve, expand, and modernize the business.

Criteria	Option 1	Option 2	Option 3	Option 4
	For all of Latin American Region as a whole with headquarters staff support	Do it for each country but with greater emphasis depending on the particulars of that country	Option 2 plus headquarters staff support	Centralize the modernization of the small countries and decentralize for each particular large country
Absolutely must, without fail:				
1. Achieve a minimum of $10 million incremental sales from modernization and repair				
2. Achieve a minimum of $3 million incremental margin by December 30, annually				
Also should:				
3.				
4.				
5.				

132

invested several hours in the task, two other teams were given tasks. One was given responsibility to conduct an Option Analysis for meeting the Field Engineering requirements. The other tackled the Human Resources and Training issues related to the modernization.

On the last day of the conference, everyone reconvened to review and troubleshoot the Communication and Implementation Plans, to discuss questions, and to agree on further refinements. Finally, task teams were created, typically with a mix of home office and country managers in order to build teamwork and apply the best know-how and experience to ensure success of each major project.

WRITTEN FEEDBACK ON IN WHAT RESPECTS, IF ANY, THE CONFERENCE *EXCEEDED* EXPECTATIONS

- "We have achieved a common vision, out of all the emotion that could have occurred. It permits us to have now and in the future a new way to face problems."
- "This process exceeded my expectations in team building, common viewpoints/lack of defensiveness/objective orientation and increased sensitivity to others' perceptions."
- "This process gave us a clear perception by all participants of the differences between some staff and line managers, or between Brazil and customers, in the perception of the quality. Rapid recuperation after the first 'shock' [of the Feedback] and in the process of teamwork."
- "This process expedited action, and indicated solutions to several major problem areas—which otherwise may have either been delayed or arbitrarily solved."

Jean Pierre's leadership of LAR, using as a key managing tool the Root Cause, Option Analysis and Risk Analysis processes, was so successful that Brazil became a dependable supplier, LAR gained market share, and he was promoted 2 years later to become president of one of the major worldwide companies.

* * *

While the Latin American Region of this company was using Option Analysis to determine the best way to modernize and compete more effectively, 3,000 miles away in Europe, another manager from a very different type of company faced the same problem of uniting a disparate management group in the goal of achieving a common cause. We'll find out in the next chapter what happened at Transnational, a multimillion-dollar global manufacturing company.

CHAPTER EIGHT

Option Analysis in Action—5: Developing a Basic Global Strategy

The recently appointed vice-president of Transnational's Manufacturing, Bill Marko, sat staring out his office window at the mist rising from the courtyard pond, musing on what he had learned in his first 4 months on the job. Here's what he had to consider:

For more than 20 years, European Manufacturing had apparently reacted to do everything it had been asked to do. There had been a succession of U.S. managers at the top, with his predecessor having further complicated things by continuing the traditional adversarial relationship with the field. Marko believed that the plants should stand on their own two feet. Although this got people to think and become somewhat independent, it just further perpetuated European Manufacturing's adversarial relationship with Sales. This was but one of many problems that would have to be resolved by building a unified corporate strategy.

THE TROUBLE WITH SUCCESS

The manufacturing operation in Europe came about as a natural outcome of a plan to make products cheaply in offshore tax havens. An initial plant was started with a very limited product range, the intent being to supply product from the United States to meet European sales needs. The intent was also to load the plan to the limit of tax advantage, but only as a small piece of global manufacturing capacity.

As European sales grew, however, supply logistics became bigger and more complex. The resultant decrease in customer satisfaction caused European operations to demand increasing control over their manufacturing supply lines. This intensified as several more plants were acquired and built, and a Business Center was established to bridge European sales needs to U.S. supply lines. Overall supply and capacity planning remained under control of U.S. Manufacturing.

Surging European business continued to force Manufacturing to concentrate on servicing the European Region. Interim measures did not solve the basic problem, and a decision was made to shift Manufacturing supply planning for Europe from the United States to Brussels in order to align it with European sales demand.

With Marko on board, European Manufacturing was given the mission of controlling and supplying (although not producing) products for all European sales needs. This included a 5-year plan based on the premise that "product should be made and service centers established in those countries where we sell." This gave rise to a significant Manufacturing presence in Europe due to:

1. Considerable experience demonstrating that European customers could not be satisfied using worldwide supply lines. Service was too slow, and order filling was inflexible and cumbersome without unacceptably high levels of

pipeline inventory. Flexibility of supply was deemed essential to achieve customer satisfaction.

2. With the coming European Economic Community (EEC), it was necessary to demonstrate value by adding to capability. It was agreed that gaining market share would be more difficult, and in some countries impossible to achieve, if the company did not visibly contribute to the economic self-sufficiency of the EEC.

Of course, this required a high level of technical capability in European Manufacturing operations beyond that simply needed for service to support sales. Given the cross-European framework of the growing business, Manufacturing capacities and technical capabilities were planned on a pan-European basis.

Consequently, within European Manufacturing, technical capabilities were increased to match those in U.S. Manufacturing. As an increasing number of U.S. manufacturers have discovered in serving European customers, being part manufacturer and part pass-through supplier of products produced elsewhere in the world has proved inefficient. As each new product is introduced, the content of that product produced in Europe is reduced because process and vendor development typically take place where the product is first built, and experience favors U.S. plants. Thus, to the extent that European Manufacturing did not develop processes and vendors concurrently with the U.S. Manufacturing operation, it became dependent on suppliers from the United States and elsewhere. Senior management realized that this would be unacceptable in the EEC and the company would consequently lose orders and market share.

Technical capabilities were added to European operations, increasing Manufacturing's value-added level. This, in turn, facilitated partnerships in design engineering work, as the company shifted toward local design of products since it recognized that in order to develop their own economies, European nations must add value to the finished goods and services they consume. Thus it adopted a "Sales, Assembly, and Manufacturing" strategy to add local content or participation and to become more European customer-friendly and competitive.

3. In view of the EEC, strategic alliances became a significant new direction for adding value in the marketplace and fueling further growth. Experimental relationships were established with several companies to enhance Manufacturing's capability and become a full-fledged member of a European business team.

    Customer satisfaction, viability in the EEC market, and the role of Manufacturing in business partnerships in turn required as high a level of investment in Manufacturing's infrastructure as possible. This was vital for achieving strategic capability in Europe and, hopefully, achieving a sustainable competitive advantage.

Overall, the objective for European Manufacturing was to become self-sufficient. Also, to become a world-class performer, global interdependence would be necessary. As in the EEC, Manufacturing would also have a supply role to other regions.

It was felt that, through such strategies, market share could double in 2 years and the company would be seen in Europe as a European company. This meant that the corporation would now depend on European manufacturing like never before, which would give Europe higher priority in competing for scarce corporate resources.

To succeed at this, Europe would need to win an increased share of corporate resources at the expense of Manufacturing's growth rate in the United States. Such resources would be needed in process and product development, technology and supplier development, business process development, and the development of people (predominantly Europeans) to meet anticipated challenges.

This, in turn, would require:

1. Extensive Human Resources development in Europe.
2. Identification and mobilization of relevant technologies in Europe.
3. Business success resulting in high levels of customer satisfaction and acceptable profitability.
4. Successful integration of Product and Regional plans— and their execution.
5. Efficient backward vertical integration.
6. Successful process and product investment.
7. Use of world-class management methods.

As in all successful enterprises, *structure* would need to follow *strategy* if success was to be achieved. The structural elements of function, geography, and product, however, had not been rationalized in European Manufacturing. The plants, for example, were set up to follow product structures and had only a loosely defined relationship to geographical subsidiaries. Although they contained all the Manufacturing staff functions, the role of these functions varied from control to support, with no explicit game plan. This product-dominant arrangement had been reinforced over a period of years. Some central resources existed to source the elements of the Region and functions, but only haphazardly, resulting more from events than by design.

All of the preceding forces suggested the need for structural change in European Manufacturing, with reduced decentralized product focus and a more balanced emphasis on central/regional resources to allow regional/product integration. The goal was to develop plant/product management and central/regional management in a way that would unify and harmonize the entire organization. The staff functions would have to become *facilitators* to accomplish this in contrast with their more controlling and dominating influence. These were the issues facing Bill Marko in his new job.

AN EXECUTIVE CHALLENGE

As Bill Marko discovered, throughout the European Manufacturing organization there was no clearly articulated and accepted mission and strategy. The "strategy" had simply been for local plant managers to take whatever action was necessary. The organizational structure was extremely complex, as Marko belatedly recognized by making the mistake, a couple of times, of championing something himself and finding, on both occasions, the absence of buy-in from his 14 subordinates (not all of whom reported directly to him).

All told, Europe consisted of eight country managers, reporting to two general managers and a European functional staff of Sales, Service, Marketing, Finance and Administration, MIS, and so forth. Each country had its own Sales, Service, Local Marketing, Finance and Administration, MIS, and Logistics departments. And Marko had inherited a functional staff of nine people.

Transnational had about 12,000 employees in Europe, with 2,400 in the Manufacturing operations. Marko's direct staff consisted of a German, an Italian, a Briton, and a Belgian, in addition to five Americans whom he was committed to replace with Europeans as soon as he could. Marko recognized that until he could get the mission and strategy resolved and bought into throughout European Manufacturing, he would not be able to determine how best to pull Manufacturing people together, let alone integrate them with the Region's field people. (The country managers, of course, were his internal company customers.)

Marko felt that he was doing all the "right things"—getting around to all the operations, managing by flying and walking around, meeting managers and employees for meals to try to pull them together as a team, and so on. Yet it seemed that everywhere he turned, he was frustrated by the U.S. Home Office and his own plant managers' inability to cut across cultural, national, and corporate hierarchical barriers to develop a viable strategy.

The cultural differences between Europeans and Americans were simply not understood back home. One difference Marko had found was that people on the Continent did not forget their history, whereas the U.S. "gung ho" attitude was "Oh, sure; the second world war was fought 50 years ago; it's a new ballgame now," and were constantly frustrated because the Europeans never seemed to change their attitude. "You simply can't force things through with the Europeans," his predecessor had advised Marko.

Marko recognized that the home office's previous "colonial attitude" (i.e., investments in Europe and elsewhere are made as extensions of Home Office's needs) had changed to one of looking at Europe as an entity in itself to build a much higher percentage of "content" to serve its country clients.

Too many Americans on the other side of the pond, however, did not act according to this strategy. The attitude frequently was, "What are the Europeans doing for us these days?" In contrast, Marko was convinced that the proper attitude now should be, "What's the right thing to do for our global business?"

Early in the game, Marko, his plant managers, and the Brussels staff had spent several days off-site working the issue of teamwork. It hadn't gone well. In fact, Marko had received a good deal of negative feedback from the whole group—that he was "emotional," "very intimidating," "much too control-oriented," "throws lightning bolts that close off issues and discussion," "stares people down when he's angry."

Marko felt that he had benefited from this feedback and realized that he was turning people off by pushing too hard. So he backed off and said he would seek much greater participation and buy-in from managers on the important things. He also recognized that he would have to work with the plants and not try to force his—or anyone's—ideas on them, and the plants would have to learn the same thing. This meant that they would have to unify around one purpose. This was especially crucial since, because of cultural differences and prejudices, any setback was amplified, multiplied, and impacted other things going on. The plants seemed only to "tolerate" the Brussels staff and, although they used them on occasion, they really didn't feel they had much value.

There were also some extremely difficult decisions to be made, strategically and tactically, such as "Should they shut down certain plants and shift certain products from other plants?" But even more important was the issue, "How can I develop and implement a viable growth strategy that will more effectively use Manufacturing and related functions as a competitive weapon, especially given that my staff is largely headed here in Brussels by Americans while our major plant operations are headed up by strong Nationals in five European countries?"

After considering these and other comments, Marko was able to obtain buy-in from his 14 plant managers and Brussels staff representing eight different nationalities that they needed to crystallize their best thinking as a *team* on what the key issues were facing European Manufacturing. As one manager had put it, "We're about to take our small craft into very rough waters, so first we have to learn how to trim the sails. Let's get in the vehicle, put our seat belts on, relax, and figure out where we're going and how we're going to get there."

Marko recognized that he would have to lead his Manufacturing organization "over the mountains," and he put out a memo announcing a project to "smoke out the issues" through a professional third party who would interview all 15 managers as well as a representative sample of relevant regional and home office managers.

Following these interviews and notification by the consultant that the findings were ready for presentation, Marko selected two plant managers and two from his Brussels staff to accompany him on a visit to the head office that would include a long, intensive day receiving feedback from the 50-plus interviews conducted on both sides of the Atlantic.

The core group identified as high-priority concerns the following:

1. *Relationship with Corporate.* There is a "parent-child" relationship in which European Manufacturing is viewed as a teenager. The feeling that home office has about Europe seems to be: "I taught you how to drive; now go drive the car, but I'll keep the keys!" As a result, European Manufacturing harbors considerable resentment at the home office's attitude and treatment.

   The home office feels that European manufacturing should take much more of a global stance. Until now, European Manufacturing was expected to take a Regional stance—but no longer, since the corporation is committed to becoming a world-class manufacturer. (In fact, some at the home office view European Manufacturing as isolationist.) The home office also wants European Manufacturing to look at itself as a piece of the global manufacturing equation, then faults it when it acts European. Yet they're supposed to also act as a Region, so are they entitled to be parochial?

   It's obvious that both the home office and European Manufacturing are confused about European Manufacturing's role. The problem with the home office is that it's a very young parent in its attitude and treatment of European Manufacturing. In response, the home office

143

says that European Manufacturing has a strong role to play in educating it—but then it doesn't listen!

2. *Mission, Common Vision, and Strategy.* There is agreement that for Europe to meet its regional goals, it must control more of what it manufactures; but once the home office raises economy-of-scale arguments, European Manufacturing caves in. Yet, European Manufacturing has so much more strength to document its case. For instance, it could lower its break-even point, but economy-of-scale thinking doesn't recognize and appreciate the value of this. European Manufacturing is therefore treated by the home office as a cost center, not a profit center.

   Does the home office truly see European Manufacturing as a cost center and not an investment? European Manufacturing feels that it can always be allowed to decide to reduce costs, but not to increase profits. It feels restricted by having to accept the home office's rules such as the establishment of gross margin levels.

   The question is, if European Manufacturing tied more into the Region, would this be more effective? Yet, what would it have to give up in the way of autonomy?

   The "drive shaft" for Europe is *customer satisfaction.* Yet, there clearly is a lack of clarity on the Mission and the Vision because so much has not been written down, such as the arrangement of priorities. No wonder managers feel disoriented and there is such a vast discrepancy in perceptions. Also, since European Manufacturing perceptions are not unified, it's not surprising that the home office sees things differently from the way European Manufacturing does. Under these circumstances, you can't expect the home office to see European Manufacturing as it views itself.

3. *Organization Structure.* Europe (the field) has too much of a Product management mindset, but there may be other

ways than this to manage the business more effectively. There is also some strong feeling that European Manufacturing needs to have an integrated position in Europe with sales and marketing but lacks sufficient resources.

It would probably be better if European Manufacturing were tied more closely (i.e., restructured) to the region; but some managers question whether Manufacturing is really even required!

In other words, there certainly isn't a common vision about what is the "organization preference." A set of criteria is truly necessary to determine the best way to organize and allocate resources.

Are there only a few who believe there should be European Manufacturing? Maybe the plants should report directly to the Product Groups. In fact, how and at what level should European Manufacturing interface and integrate with the Product Groups?

Answering this question requires resolving and communicating answers to an additional set of questions: (a) What's the business reason for European Manufacturing's existence? (b) What should the level of integration of European Manufacturing be; for instance, should it be integrated with Marketing and Engineering? (c) What should the best organization structure be? (d) If we integrate, what degree of control will we have over our own destiny—will we be gobbled up by the Region?

4. *Team Effectiveness.* Many of the managers interviewed from European Manufacturing are obviously participating silently at meetings. This is evident by the realization that so many of the concerns that Marko and his small group of managers thought had long since been put to bed are still being debated. Apparently, there is no commitment to agreements when they are reached. Silence has been interpreted to mean agreement, but apparently

it very often isn't. Why else is there so much diversity of opinion and perceptions—so much disarray?

5. *The Plants and the Plant Manager Role.* There is a perception that the plants have too much power. The plant manager is seen as the "rattle," which suggests a great lack of trust in that he is not part of the team. And there certainly is a Brussels functional staff versus plant manager conflict. This discussion about the role of the Brussels' staff functions vis-à-vis the plant manager has occurred several times; why is it still an issue?

There's also a perception around the role of the plant and plant manager, around productivity, and around expansion of the several European plants that's very different from the perceptions of these particular plant managers. Therefore, we need to understand where people get such perceptions. How can these misperceptions be dispelled? Obviously, a process is needed that facilitates performance review and gets everyone on the same wavelength with regard to the facts. This, in turn, requires that people must feel secure enough to express their judgments honestly, and once agreement is reached, it's got to be committed to and executed.

Once and for all, the responsibility of the plant manager vis-à-vis the staff functions vis-à-vis European manufacturing vis-à-vis the Region needs to be defined. The plants are product-focused, so it's difficult to push them into having a pan-European program. That's at least in part why there is the perception of "You need to 'de-power' the plants—or take the product focus away from them."

Are there only a few managers like Marko who believe there should be European Manufacturing? Maybe the plants should report directly to the Product Groups. How and at what level should European Manufacturing interface and integrate with the Product Groups? Does the Field in Europe even appreciate what it can gain from European Manufacturing?

6. *Decision Making.* The decision-making process is not formal enough. Although there is much discussion, obviously there is little commitment. Marko must make decisions and his managers "go with them." People, however, don't express their concerns, nor do they honor decisions made.

European Manufacturing does need a common vision and articulated strategies. Marko is now trying to be too participative. And managers expect *him* to resolve these issues. Instead, the issue should be, "How can Marko best put the monkey on *everyone's* back to resolve them?"

Less than a week after beginning the process, Marko convened his 15 managers in Vuarnet to receive 100 percent of the same Feedback Report and presentation which he had received in Chicago. After an intensive day and a half of review and prioritization of the issues, the group boiled the more than 150 issues down to 5 essential ones!

Descending Order of Vote

1. Need for a *common vision* of Mission, Goals, and Strategy. [15 votes]

   Note: Vision and Strategy include European self-sufficient supply, and the Regional Manufacturing Strategy vis-à-vis the Field and Corporate. Need to clarify also the Vision of 1992 and then communicate this.

2. Leadership/Teamwork and Decision Making. [14 votes]

   We need to develop a decision-making process that helps us develop teamwork and helps us know when we have agreement and when we don't.

   We must learn better how to work together to avoid

such diversity of opinion in the future. What will it take to build a true team? This requires trust. But can we really get the level of trust that is required? Trust is required to develop unanimity of agreement on the Mission and regarding integration with the Region.

3. Organization Structure. [11 votes]

    We need to define and implement the organization in its integration with the Region (i.e., vis-à-vis Field, Engineering, and even European industry).

    This includes defining the team we want to be in order to operate the business, given what we agree on as our direction and strategy.

4. Communication and Interaction. [6 votes]

    We need to develop a communication process and communication strategy for European Manufacturing, for Corporate, and for the Region in order to ensure closure on decisions and effective communication in the future.

    This involves developing areas of common perception and objectives in respect to European Manufacturing.

5. Roles and Relationships, and Responsibility/Authority/Accountability. [5 votes]

    We need to define the roles and relationships of functional groups in terms of operational management within European Manufacturing, nailing down and implementing the respective degree of responsibility/authority/accountability within and between functions and the plants. This must include delineation of the *approval process* for the many decisions involved in the way we analyze the business and our key relationships with one another, with customers and vendors, with the Region and Field, and with the home office.

Ten days later, the group eagerly met in Davos to grapple with as many of these issues as five and a half days would permit. Marko opened the conference by stating:

- All manufacturing in our corporation is in trouble. There's an ongoing debate about the Regions and functional management continuing as is, and this is heightened by the establishment of a new Region.
- There is a really big question as to who owns the plants— the Product groups or the Functions?
- We have a major budgetary problem, as we are spending more as a European manufacturer than we can afford.
- I'm not sure how long we have to settle some of these questions in general manufacturing. There is a good chance that time is going to run out on me and us. So "the boat" could get called in at any time. If so, I'm afraid we may have to go back to a centralized Manufacturing function, etc.
- If we feel strongly about maintaining the Regional and European Manufacturing concepts, we must press on. This week is therefore extremely important to us. There is so much we have to accomplish, so how well we work together is going to be critical, and how well we resolve the issues will make a big difference.

Because so much was at stake for the managers, the corporation, and the customers and people, Marko asked the managers to try to anticipate what could interfere with the productivity of the work and then to develop ground rules to avoid this.

Ground rules for analysis of the issues were then developed and agreed on, including:

1. We have agreed that this conference will be a "danger-free" environment. That means, *what* we say stays here; *who* said what stays here.

2. We need to especially *listen well* and respect what each other is saying as meaningful for that person.
3. We must define where we are going to collaborate and where and against whom we will compete.
4. Let's focus on maximizing profits for European Manufacturing and the corporation.
5. We need to understand what we're going to be doing—the context and content—and *agree on objectives.*
6. Don't stop with the first solution to a problem.
7. Once we decide on a path, have each other say what it is to ensure mutual understanding and commitment. Recognize what tradeoffs may be required (i.e., *who* may have to give up *what*).

Given the priority issues agreed on at the Feedback Session, the group discussed these briefly and then agreed that a major decision had to be reached by the end of the conference: "What would be the best way to significantly strengthen European Manufacturing's long-term contribution to the total Region's business?"

Since everyone in the room had some opinion about the answer, Marko suggested that they apply the formal seven-step Option Analysis process. He described this process as, first and foremost, a "thinking things through" discipline as well as a simple yet powerful vehicle for productive dialogue.

After generating an extensive list of possible criteria for what various members of the group felt needed to be *achieved*, *preserved*, and *avoided* by the best ways, the managers prioritized these, agreeing on a number of Absolute Requirements, such as:

1. Comply with 1992 regulations.
2. Avoid any deterioration whatsoever in the current level of our Sourcing Charter.
3. Meet today's European financial budget.
4. Avoid any deterioration whatsoever in customer satisfaction standards both during and after transition.

5. Avoid any deterioration whatsoever in new product shipping release dates.

Their agreed-on Desirable Objectives included:

6. Maximize customer satisfaction.
7. Achieve greater capacity.
8. Achieve an integrated P&L with the field.
9. Achieve a high probability that Europe will be perceived as an investment center rather than as a cost center.
10. Achieve products more adapted for Europe.
11. Achieve faster reaction to changes in the external environment.
12. Achieve accelerated TTM (Time to Market).

Just the process of specifying and agreeing on the criteria (Step 3) and then on their priorities (Step 4) served to wire the team together. As a result, the managers easily generated possible options for meeting their criteria (Step 5). The options were wide-ranging, and included:

1. Have European Operations take more direct responsibility and accountability for Manufacturing (which at that time was very much under the control of the profit centers headquartered in the United States).
2. Integrate all the functions through local geographies (the "country" model).
3. Combine Manufacturing and Corporate logistics.
4. Have each European plant report directly to the relevant product group in the United States, with European Operations disappearing.
5. Have the plant report directly to the European Manufacturing function.

For the next 2 days, a healthy dialogue ensued during which each option was evaluated against the final 6 Absolute Requirements and 24 Desirable Objectives. The extensive set of criteria was warranted by the complexity of the issue and magnitude of its impact, and to reflect the beliefs and judgments of the 8 nationalities represented by the 15 managers.

Phone calls, telexes, and faxes went back and forth from the conference center to Brussels and various manufacturing plants and field offices in the United States and Europe, speeding up the whole decision-making process; the stakes were high—millions of dollars and 2,400 jobs in European Manufacturing, not to mention hundreds, if not thousands, more in the Region and at the home office!

After five and a half days, the group left, exhausted but satisfied that they had put together a workable plan. But what came out of the decision-making conference was more than a plan—it was a means for significantly strengthening European Operations and building bonds between all the European and U.S. management groups.

Marko summed up the conference: "The way we've all worked together with this decision process has put to rest a lot of misconceptions, poor attitudes, ghosts, and fears that in the past have hampered our progress. I'm delighted at the healthy teamwork we've built this week through good and open communication. And we've now got a road map for future thinking and analysis. It certainly has instilled discipline without the loss of spontaneity; our discussions have been crisp and to the point. I also believe we've achieved far greater mutual respect for one another so that we can serve each other better. We finally have a team process, which should strengthen our competitiveness. While the progress at this meeting is only a first step, we've laid a firm foundation that should ensure our viability and ability to grow the business in Europe to our 1996 goal.

"The key to why we worked so much better here was that we used a structure, provided by the process. Such things as coming in on time, not tolerating side conversations, process checks, having a scribe, etc., helped us make tremendous progress. We still need more ground rules and process aids like starting each meeting with what kind of meeting it will be;

evaluating the impact of a decision for its implications; and using issues and criteria driving our decision to help us communicate it to people. Three specific managers will be the 'Process Guardians,' including at the next general meeting in three months.

"Finally, we all have to navigate. But in one boat, not as a fleet."

On the whole, the group members were exuberant that they had succeeded in focusing 15 sets of business beliefs, values, feelings, objectives, attitudes, and judgments on a major and extremely complex issue and had arrived at 100 percent consensus. Many pointed to the ground rules as a being a key element of success—and even asked for more to help resolve future issues.

What resulted when the Action Program was marketed and communicated to the Region, Field, and home office? Several major pieces of European Operations were melded with the Region, streamlining the organizational structure and achieving not only greater efficiency and productivity, but greater customer satisfaction. As just one example, the "back end" of the country organization, Administrative Logistics (with 1,500 employees), which receives the shipped product, was folded into European Manufacturing, which was renamed "European Operations" so that logistics and manufacturing became totally integrated. Many of the staff functions of European Manufacturing were also melded with the Region.

The bottom line is one entire pipeline from vendor to customer—and a European Region that now is the biggest profit contributor to this world-class manufacturer.

PART III

Risk Analysis

CHAPTER NINE

$$\infty$$

Risk Analysis

When Frank Guggenheim turned 45, he experienced something that many of us have already faced (or will face in the future): a major change in careers. Guggenheim, an assistant manager of a medium-sized hotel in Hartford, and his wife, Anne, knew the decision would have a major impact on their lives. With several job offers, as well as the possibility of starting a consulting business, Frank and Anne used Option Analysis to determine the most appropriate course of action. After evaluating several options against the criteria they set, the clear winner turned out to be not only a job move for Frank, but a geographical relocation over 1,500 miles away! "Could this really be the right decision?" Frank asked himself.

To find out for certain whether Frank and Anne should move to the Caribbean, the two needed to conduct a Risk Analysis of the options. In the previous chapters, we've seen Root Cause Analysis and Option Analysis in a number of contexts. Now it's time to introduce the third component of the *Complete Thought Process: Risk Analysis*. Risk Analysis is really Causal Analysis *before* the fact—that is, anticipating what can go wrong (or right), where it can go wrong (or right), and when it can go wrong (or right).

THE PROCESS

Step 1

Scan for and specify potential risks that may be inherent in or created by your decision or action. Ask yourself, "What are all the things that can go wrong [and, to look opportunistically, can go *right*] with this decision or action?" List them, without judging their feasibility, realism, and so forth.

Step 2

The next step is to prioritize. Obviously, there may be some pitfalls that your gut feel says you cannot afford to risk. Let's analyze how your gut knows this.

If you think about it, risk is really a function of two factors. The first is the impact or severity of each risk, each potential problem. In other words, what would be the consequences of a particular roadblock to your decision, plan, or action if it did indeed happen? (You can use a simple weighing system—High, Medium, and Low—to reflect the potential severity of each one.) The second factor is chance or probability of occurrence. It makes sense to assess every High (or even Medium) risk in terms of the likelihood of its occurring. (Again, you can use High, Medium, and Low to reflect your judgment.) The second step therefore involves assessing the risks in terms of Impact and Chance.

Step 3

Whether you decide to tackle just the high-impact and probability risks, or all of them, you must first determine why each risk would occur in the first place. Let's take a simple example with which you are familiar: Can you prevent a fire? If you say "Yes," you're wrong! In reality, you can only try to prevent the likely *causes* of a fire, such as smoking, campfires that get out of hand, household chemicals, and so forth. That's because fires don't just start; something, somewhere, at some specific point in time—each of the three of some scope or magnitude—causes a fire to start (i.e., lightning, careless smokers, etc.).

Pinpointing the most probable cause is Step 3. This is not as easy as it sounds, because any event, condition, or situation can be caused by more than one other event; since it could occur in the future, more than one likely cause could create its existence. So it's important to identify the likely causes of *each* risk and then home in on the ones that really concern you (the ones with the highest probability).

Step 4

This step is to think through whether there is anything that can be done to prevent each risk. In most situations, however, before you can identify specific preventive actions that realistically can be taken to remove the likelihood of a potential risk's causing a problem, you must figure out each likely cause that could, in turn, create the higher-level causes of the problem. For example, excessive heat (a lower-level cause) might cause certain chemicals to ignite, causing a fire.

Step 5

Once you've identified specific, timely, and economical preventive actions, it's time to take Step 5 and specify protective actions that minimize the seriousness of your high potential risks, should they occur despite your preventive efforts. Let's say you tried to prevent one likely cause of a fire by putting up "No Smoking" signs in a warehouse. Somehow, someone ignored the sign and dropped a lighted cigarette on the floor, starting a fire. Your preventive action ("No Smoking" signs) has failed; what's left to be activated is your protective action (which, in this case, hopefully would be a sprinkler system).

One way to differentiate protective from preventive action is that the protective action is set up ahead of time to take effect if the potential risk occurs to minimize the impact (and, in this case, put out the fire). Protective actions are usually more expensive than preventive actions, since they invariably have to be set up and may require maintenance over time. They also require some type of monitoring system to scan for trouble, recognize when it happens, and sound the alarm or initiate a corrective process.

Preventive action, on the other hand, reduces the likelihood that a cause will happen in the first place—which is where the real payoff usually is.

The other side of the coin is opportunistic (instead of preventive) action, which is taken to bring one or more likely causes into existence so that they *create* the potential opportunity.

Step 6

The sixth, and last, step in Risk Analysis is to look at what you are developing in terms of a Communication and Implementation Plan for your decision. Doing so will raise the probability that your decision and actions will indeed achieve your targeted results.

PUTTING RISK ANALYSIS TO WORK

Before you read about some actual applications related to global business, let's take a more mundane example. What could go wrong with a construction company's putting a dynamite shed in woods nearby its new development?

Step 1   Specify potential risks—or opportunities.

Step 2   Prioritize each potential risk or opportunity, assessing its impact and chance of occurrence.

Step 3   Specify Likely Causes (and their own likely causes).

Step 4   Specify preventive action against each lowest-level specific Likely Cause to reduce the probability of its occurring, causing the chain reaction leading to the risk actually occurring. Similarly, specify opportunistic actions against each lowest-level Likely Cause to increase the probability of its occurring.

Step 5   Specify protective actions against each major potential risk.

Step 6   Refine the plan or develop a Communication and Implementation Plan.

Both the Option and Risk (and Opportunity) Analysis processes are easily applicable to personal decisions as well as to professional and business decisions. The steps may feel awkward at first, and may seem time-consuming. But once you begin using them, they should enable you to speed up your decision making and raise the probability of achieving targeted results.

The two processes should also help you make stronger, more-effective decisions, save you a great deal of time and money, increase the probability of successful implementation, and give you far greater security and peace of mind in your decisions and plans.

THE CARIBBEAN LURE

Let's return to our friend Frank Guggenheim, and see how he and his wife used Risk Analysis to confirm that they had selected the right option.

"Okay, Anne," Frank said to his wife, "If we have agreed

that we should move down to the Caribbean and I should accept the night manager job at the resort, then how can we ensure that, when I announce what were going to do and we do it, things go smoothly and don't get bollixed up?"

"One of the first things I have learned at work," Anne replied, "is that given our decision, we should identify the potential risks that could occur by asking ourselves, 'What are all the things that could go wrong with this decision?'"

"That's a good idea, Anne. Let's do it. To start off, I think one potential risk is that we won't be able to sell our house, given the recession and the glut in the housing market here in the Northeast."

"That really concerns me, too. I'm also worried that I won't be able to find a job when I decide to go back into the workplace once Frank, Jr., is a little older."

As Frank and Anne started listing all the things that could go wrong with their decision, it very quickly became apparent that implementing their decision was no small task. In addition to the risks they just came up with, there were various other potential risks, as revealed in the following summary.

Step 1: Scanning for and Specifying Potential Risks

1. We may not be able to sell our house fast enough.
2. Anne may not be able to find employment when she re-enters the workplace.
3. Both of our sets of parents may not approve of such a faraway move and may feel hurt by our decision.
4. The discussion with my boss may go badly when I give my notice.
5. We may not have the proper wardrobe for a year-round warm climate.
6. There may not be adequate daycare or schooling for Frank, Jr.
7. We may not have enough money to buy the kind of house we are used to.

8. There may not be enough going on culturally to keep us satisfied.
9. We may not be accepted by the Island people and may have trouble making new friends.
10. We may not like living in a resort community.
11. My grandmother may want to spend the winter with us instead of in Florida.
12. I may not like working nights.
13. They may not let our dog, Reggae, on the island.

"You know, Anne," said Frank, "we identified all these dangers in only 5 minutes! I'm not even sure we have got them all. That's kind of frightening! But maybe we should deal with all of these first before listing any others."

"Okay," said Anne, "but instead of dealing with all of them, let's try to evaluate them in terms of how serious each of these risks would be if it were to happen, and in terms of its chance of occurring. Then we can use a high, medium, and low weighting technique, first addressing those risks that are both high severity and high likelihood. That way, we'll make the best use of our time."

"Great idea!" Frank replied as he and Anne began assessing the impact and chance of each potential risk's occurring.

Step 2: Prioritize—Assess Impact and Chance of Potential Risks (High/Medium/Low)

1. We may not be able to sell our house fast enough. [High Impact, High Chance—HH]
2. Anne won't be able to find employment when she re-enters the workplace. [HL]
3. Both of our sets of parents may not approve of such a faraway move and may feel hurt by our decision. [MM]
4. The discussion with my boss may go badly when I give my notice. [HH]
5. We may not have the proper wardrobe for a year-round warm climate. [LH]

6. There may not be adequate daycare or schooling for Frank, Jr. [HM]
7. We may not have enough money to buy the kind of house we are used to. [MM]
8. There may not be enough going on culturally to keep us satisfied. [ML]
9. We may not be accepted by the Island people and may have trouble making new friends. [HL]
10. We may not like living in a resort community. [HL]
11. My grandmother may want to spend the winter with us instead of in Florida. [HL]
12. I may not like working nights. [HM]
13. They may not let our dog, Reggae, on the island. [ML]

As Frank scanned over the prioritized list he and Anne had developed, his eyes kept focusing on one particular high impact/high probability potential risk.

"You know," Anne, "I'm really worried about the meeting I've got to have with my boss. Telling Don that I am going to be leaving the company after 7 years there—and during our busiest time of the year—really makes it very difficult."

"Boy," said Anne, "I really don't envy your having to tell Don, because I know how much he has been counting on you. After all, he has treated us very well."

"That's right. And I also don't want to burn my bridges. You know my position with this company can really help me when, and if, we ever decide to move back here. My seeking employment back at the company sometime in the future also isn't out of the question, so it's important that my meeting go really well."

"Well," said Anne, "let's see what could cause your meeting with Don to go poorly. What can we think of that is likely to cause the meeting not to meet your objectives?"

As a guide to help smoke out the risks, Frank was already thinking in terms of what he wanted to achieve, avoid, and preserve during his meeting with Don. "Don could feel betrayed by my leaving. I've always been the one he can count on."

Anne quickly replied, "This is also the busiest time of year. I think the hectic pace at work could cause Don either not to listen or to get angry at you due to the pressure of the business."

"You're probably right, Anne. The hectic pace of the business might be a likely cause of Don's getting angry or not listening to me—either of which could cause my meeting to go badly. While I can't do much about the hectic pace of the business right now, I can take some preventive action against both Don's being angry and Don's not listening. But I guess the next step is to add these three to our list of likely causes of my meeting's going poorly."

Frank and Anne continued developing their list of likely reasons for the meeting with Don not to go well:

Step 3: List Likely Causes
1. Don may feel betrayed and angry.
2. Don may not listen to me.
3. Bad timing due to the hectic pace of the business.
4. Don could be interrupted before I say everything I need to.
5. Don could be pressured for time.
6. I could "chicken out" and not give my notice.
7. Don could convince me to stay.

When they finished the list, Anne asked, "Which of these seven really bother you?"

"Every single one!"

"Okay, then I guess you've done the prioritizing—they're all top priority! Now what we need to do is think of some preventive actions that will reduce the chances of each of the Likely Causes from happening. For example, if we look at the first one on our list [Don may feel betrayed and angry], we need to ask ourselves, 'What action can you take to prevent

165

this from happening?' Or do we need to drive it one step lower and think of why Don would feel betrayed and angry?"

"Let's drive it lower. For example, Don could feel angry because he may not understand my rationale. Or he may feel overwhelmed because of the increase in workload he's got to take on with my departure."

"So what can you do about these two reasons, Frank?"

"One thing I should do to prevent this from happening is make sure I let him know how much I value our relationship and give him some background on our decision, maybe even show him the criteria we came up with so he understands our reasons and how carefully we have thought things through. At least this way he'd hopefully agree that, for us, it makes a lot of sense. And since I believe he likes and respects me, I think it would reduce or even prevent his anger or feeling over-whelmed. Also, I need to make sure I give him as much notice as possible. In fact, if I talk to him by the end of next week, then I could really give him 4 full week's notice and still leave us time to do everything else we have to do before I start my new position."

"Those are two good preventive actions, Frank. Now let's look at the next Likely Cause, 'Don may not listen to you.' Why not, Frank?"

"Umm, he might get interrupted by phone calls, or his secretary may knock at the door with something important, or he's got other things on his mind."

"What preventive actions can you take to reduce the likeli-hood of each of these occurring?"

"Well, I guess I could have the meeting off-hours—either an early morning appointment or the last appointment of the day. Maybe it should be a breakfast meeting or even after work over a cocktail, because he and I do have that kind of relationship."

"I think that makes good sense. And you know, that also helps you prevent one of the other Likely Causes from happen-ing which we identified: interruptions. That's killing two birds with one stone."

"Another thing I could do is to ask him how he feels about what I have said and how he understands what I tried to communicate to him. That gives me the chance to summarize, add to, or complement his understanding with anything else to further make sure he did really hear me."

"Frank, I think you've got some really first-class ideas there. I'm honestly very impressed with you! But the important thing is, how do you feel about them? Are you comfortable?"

"Yes. I really feel better. You know, by trying to reduce the chance that each of these Likely Causes will happen, I already feel more comfortable with our decision. I think that we can really see this through to meeting our expectations if I implement these ideas with Don and if we take this approach with the rest of the potential risks we have identified."

Frank and Anne continued down their list, identifying specific preventive actions against each of the Likely Causes of the meeting with Don not to go well.

Step 4: List Preventive Actions
Number 1 Likely Cause: Don may feel betrayed and angry. (Why?)

    1A Lower-level cause:
        Don may not understand the rationale.
        Preventive action:
        Give Don the background of the decision and stress how I value our relationship; show Don my criteria.

    1B Lower-level cause:
        Don may well feel overwhelmed by the increase in the workload and my unexpected resignation.
        Preventive action:
        Give 4 or even 6 weeks' notice instead of just 2 weeks.

Number 2 Likely Cause: Don may not listen to me. (Why not?)

    2A Lower-level cause:
        Don could feel pressured for time.

Preventive action:
Need to analyze for lower-level likely causes (as follows):

2B   Lower-level cause:
Daily business requirements could preoccupy his mind.
Preventive action:
Off-hours meeting (before or after work), maybe over cocktails or a breakfast meeting. Test his understanding of what I've said; ask how he feels about what I've said. (Note: This is actually a protective, rather than a preventive, action. It won't prevent Don's not wanting to really "hear" what Frank has to say. Instead, Don's responses to Frank's questions will alert Frank about whether Don is "hearing" so that he can communicate better and more convincingly.)

2C   Lower-level cause:
I could take too much time.
(Why? Because I'm not well enough prepared.)
Preventive action:
Prepare a list of objectives and key points.

2D   Lower-level cause:
Our schedules might conflict.
Preventive action:
Let Don pick the best time for him to meet with me.

2E   Lower-level cause:
Interruptions. (Why?)
   2E1   Lower-level cause:
   Phone calls.
   Preventive action:
   Have meeting in a location where there are no phones.

<pre>
    2E2 Lower-level cause:
         People could walk into the room.
         Preventive action:
         Close door; meet off-hours.
</pre>

Number 3 Likely Cause: Bad timing due to the hectic pace of the business.
Preventive action: See 1B.

Number 4 Likely Cause: Don could be interrupted before I say everything I need to.
Preventive action: See 2B, 2E2.

Number 5 Likely Cause: Don could be pressured for time.
Preventive action: See 2A, 2E2.

Number 6 Likely Cause: I could "chicken out" and not give my notice.
<pre>
    6A   Lower-level cause:
         I may not be confident about what I'm going to say.
         Preventive action:
         Dry run the meeting with Anne several times,
         including responding to several objections before
         they are even raised.
</pre>

Number 7 Likely Cause: Don could convince me to stay. (Why?)
<pre>
    7A   Lower-level cause:
         I could start listening to his biased pros and cons.
         Preventive action:
         Remember and focus on my criteria and our Option
         Analysis.
</pre>

"What are you thinking about, Frank?" Anne asked as she noticed his pensive look.

"You know, your Risk Analysis procedures are neat; I feel even more confident now that I see the same Likely Causes and preventive actions coming up more than once. That says two things: One, it sure is fortunate that we took the time to do this, because it's entirely possible that these things would have occurred and derailed our plan. Second, we've got a solid plan!"

Anne looked at their list of preventive actions proudly. "I agree, Frank. I think these will go a long way in keeping the Likely Causes from happening," she said. "Now let's take a look at the other High-Impact/High-Chance potential risks and do the same."

So Anne and Frank continued, taking their prioritized list of potential risks and listing Likely Causes of each and determining preventive actions against each. Then, they completed their Risk Analysis by refining their decision (Step 6). They were so confident that they didn't set up any protective actions (other than changing the amount of notice time).

Frank subsequently did have his meeting with Don and it went better than expected. Don expressed great disappointment, but he took the resignation well. He said he would help in any way he could, especially since Frank agreed to give 6 weeks' notice before leaving to smooth his departure's impact on the department (since 4 weeks did not sufficiently reduce Don's concern).

Today, you may see Frank and Anne if you're in St. John in the Virgin Islands, enjoying the benefits of their decision supported by their Risk Analysis.

As with Causal Analysis and Option Analysis, effective Risk (and Opportunity) Analysis requires balancing your mind and heart, integrating the feelings and thinking of everyone involved with making—and implementing—the best decision.

CHAPTER TEN

Risk Analysis in Action—1: Retaking the Hill

In the late 1980s, Greyland Enterprises, a multinational maker of machine parts, was experiencing an alarming lack of customer confidence and an erosion of business and marketplace share. With the difficult economy, customers were demanding lower prices, and at the same time, better service. A set of feedback reports based on customer and vendor interviews revealed two major weaknesses: First, customers perceived Greyland as arrogant. Customers would then take an adversarial position and not be "open" and candid with sales and service representatives, so that everyone entered meetings expecting to do battle. Second, order handling was a major source of customer irritation. In the words of Charles Walters, Greyland's new President, "Too many customers are having great difficulty doing business with us." After performing a detailed Option Analysis to strengthen the company's reputation and restore customer confidence, one option in particular (which had been #5) proved to be the winner: "Restructure the organization to place necessary decision-making authority and accountability at the customer interface level." Now Walters faced the task of conducting a Risk Analysis to determine what might go wrong with the implementation of this option.

Even though this option was the winner, it was not 15 percent greater than either of two runner-up options; in fact, those two options also made a lot of sense. So Walters and his management team concluded that perhaps they should implement all three. (Option 4 was "Assign clear responsibility and set up measuring systems to monitor performance"; option 7 was "Provide training within the entire organization to achieve employee understanding of customer relationships.")

As you can imagine, implementing just one of the options would require many actions executed with great care and precision. Implementing three of them would require a major, well-integrated effort. As you see from Tables 10.1, 10.2, and 10.3, the management team did the necessary Risk Analysis for each option separately and developed specific recommendations for a cohesive, well-thought-out Implementation Plan. (Note that the management team did not separately identify preventive action from protective action but, rather, combined them together under one column. When reviewing the tables, you can test your understanding of the difference by separating the preventive actions from the protective actions—you'll find it a useful exercise.)

> Option 5: Restructure the organization to place necessary decision-making authority and accountability at the customer interface level. (See Table 10.1.)

Analysis
- If this is a fairly major change in activities and authority, there probably are more than five potential problems, any one of which may be more significant than these (i.e., at least warranting a High/High for impact and chance).
- Second, all five are expressed as givens—as facts—whereas in reality, it is better to use the conditional "may" (for example, "We *may* not have qualified people (People *may* not understand.) (This reduces argumentation!)

Table 10.1 Option 5—Restructure the Organization to Place Necessary Decision-Making Authority and Accountability at the Customer Interface Level

Potential Risks	Impact	Probability	Preventive and Protective Action
a. We don't have qualified people to support the concept.	H	H	1. Carefully evaluate qualifications and experience of internal people and assess ability to do the *job* before assigned. 2. Hire people from outside if necessary.*
b. People in organization don't understand structure.	M	M	Train people.
c. New higher-level management is concerned with erosion of its authority.	M	H	Counsel, train, and (if necessary) reassign* personnel and responsibilities.
d. Individuals are unfamiliar with delegation principle.	H	H	Make sure people who are assigned the responsibilities are trained to solve customer problems.
e. We won't have positive "strokes" from upper management.	M	M	Management must support and reinforce the concept.

*This action is protective, not preventive.

- Walters' team did not specify likely causes. The consequence is that the Preventive Actions are general, more of a "shotgun" rather than "rifle shot," and may miss removing certain highly likely causes (i.e., simply training people doesn't ensure that they necessarily understand or even agree with the decision, nor that they will implement it effectively).

- The two asterisked (★) items are indeed protective actions. They may minimize the seriousness of the problem if it occurs, but they can't prevent it from happening. For instance, replacing a manager who feels his or her authority has been eroded and who hasn't accepted the situation doesn't prevent his or her feeling upset or dissatisfied; it merely necessitates a staffing change, with its own potential pitfalls—let alone possibly losing a competent manager.

Now let's go on. Keeping what's just been discussed in mind, see what you think of the next Risk Analysis.

Option 4: Assign clear responsibility and set up measuring systems to monitor performance. (See Table 10.2.)

Analysis
- For this option, Walters' team identified seven risks, all of them High Impact. In itself, this should be a major red flag. Yet, the team did not specify likely causes for any of the risks.

  Test this guideline yourself: You can't prevent any risk in and of itself; you can only remove each of the likely causes, any one of which might bring about the risk. Note also the number of asterisked (★) items, indicating that these are clearly protective, not preventive, actions. No wonder this is the trap that the team fell into: Since time was not invested in smoking out Likely Causes, people tend to jump to protective, not preventive, actions, allowing problems to occur that could have been prevented.

  The two daggered (†) items are combinations of preventive and protective actions. To the extent that such actions eliminate deterioration, they are indeed preventive. They

Table 10.2 Option 4—Assign Clear Responsibility and Set Up Measuring Systems to Monitor Performance

Potential Risks	Impact	Probability	Preventive and Protective Action
a. Monitored but no corrective action.	H	M	Find the breakdown and correct it.*
b. Monitoring system deteriorates.	H	H	Audit with selected customers twice annually by independent survey group.†
c. Assigned responsibilities not made clear.	H	M	Management must make sure objectives are clearly defined and understood.
d. Person assigned not able to handle responsibility.	H	L	Take corrective action.*
e. Bad decisions are made by an individual.	H	L	Take corrective action.*
f. People with assigned responsibilities are bypassed.	H	H	Need strong management support and effective communications system.†
g. Ineffective monitoring procedure created.	H	H	Be sure things measured will measure customer satisfaction.

*This action is protective, not preventive.
†This action is a combination preventive and protective action.

also are a warning system that reveals that things aren't working as planned, and that protective actions need to be taken as soon as possible.

Although seven risks are anticipated, there is really only one true preventive action (g) against an undesignated likely cause of an ineffective monitoring procedure's being created. And yet, being sure that these things measured will actually indicate customer satisfaction is no assurance that the monitoring procedure will work.

Likewise, item c does not ensure buy-in and commitment to the efficient execution of the manager's tasks and responsibilities.

Why are these actions so protective—rather than preventive—especially where the payoff invariably is to prevent a risk (a fire), not fight it after it's raging? There are two possible reasons for this.

First, all seven risks have been stated as facts (e.g., "Monitoring system deteriorates," "Assigned responsibilities not made clear," etc.). But not one of them *is* a fact—each is simply a hypothesis about a future potential problem that hasn't yet occurred. Just stating them as potential risks should suggest there may be more than one likely cause. Indeed, any potential risk has more than one possible cause, because it hasn't been created yet. True, some may be more probable than others, but any future event theoretically can be created by more than one possible cause.

As you've seen, the likely causes of each risk were not clearly and specifically identified before possible actions were examined. And that's what this list looks like—a series of suggested actions without a close look at their goal, which should have been to remove the likely causes of each and every significant risk.

- Stating each risk as a fait accompli almost automatically plunges you into action instead of suggesting that you first step back from the scene of the (potential) crime and anticipate its Likely Causes. All in all, it's far better to put your management time, effort, and money into addressing and preventing the High/High or High/Medium impact and chance items than "shotgunning" all of the risks identified, as this management group has done.

Option 7: Provide training within the entire organization to achieve employee understanding of customer relationships and needs. (See Table 10.3.)

Table 10.3 Option 7—Provide Training within the Entire Organization to Achieve Employee Understanding of Customer Relationships and Needs

Potential Risks	*Impact*	*Probability*	*Preventive and Protective Action*
a. Preconceived prejudices about what training will accomplish.	H	H	Program must be well thought out and clearly presented.
b. The training is incomplete.	H	H	Utilize outside facilitators if necessary.
c. Trainers don't understand customer relations.	H	M	Management must carefully select and explain the mission.
d. Training is not accomplished.	H	L	Management must free up and provide resources to be certain action is accomplished.
e. Concern for cost of quality training and time.	M	M	Develop effective training plan bought into by appropriate people.
f. Training limited to one level.	H	H	Design program(s) and timetable(s) to train all levels.
g. Management commitment not perceived.	H	M	The Corporation and Division must make it clear they support the program.
h. Existing employees have difficult in accepting new responsibility.	H	M	Ensure appraisals made before and after assignment.

Analysis

- Again, we have what looks to be a pretty good list of potential risks—eight, in fact—but some are so broad that there must be a number of Likely Causes for each. Here are some of the Likely Causes:

  d1-4 May lack sufficient numbers of personnel, let alone qualified personnel, to be trained or to provide the training.

  d5 May lack agreement that this program makes good sense.

  d6 May lack sufficient motivation.

  d7 Possibly conflicting priorities.

  d8 The reward system may not be modified to reinforce successful or superior performance.

Many of the actions identified are so broad that they may well not deal with specific Likely Causes of each major risk.

After some further fleshing out of this Risk Analysis, the management team actually developed the following Implementation Plan. (Later it further refined it into a series of columns, identifying the *task*, by *when* the action would be completed, by *whom*, and *how*.)

1. Establish project management organization in the Division to handle new unit orders from pre-order stage throughout customer acceptance. Major parts orders and revamps must fall within project management control.

2. Structure engineering (product and systems), procurement expediting, cost control, and manufacturing to support the project management concept.

3. Staff with personnel knowledgeable in project management.

4. Carefully evaluate qualifications and experience of internal people and assess ability to perform function and handle responsibility. If experience is not available, hire from outside.

5. Define and assign responsibilities throughout the organization, and establish a system to measure performance.
6. Ensure that people assigned responsibility are trained in what constitutes customer responsiveness.
7. Implement a program to demonstrate to key customers that we have changed.
    a. Review and acknowledge purchase orders within 30 days of receipt.
    b. All customer proposals must fully address the customer specifications.
    c. The president must communicate with key customers, in concert with the responsible field sales representative, concerning changes in the project execution procedures.
    d. Audit customer satisfaction on a biannual basis by an independent group.
8. Management must give strong support to the project management concept and ensure that all people work through channels so that the individuals assigned the responsibility are not bypassed.

Despite the gaps in this company's Risk Analysis, the division managers were successful in changing the culture to become more customer-responsive. The two keys to the success of the overall project were:

1. The database, which was developed from confidential interviews with customers, other key external constituencies, and the company's own managers, told them very directly which of their beliefs about their competitiveness were simply myths or wishful thinking and, specifically, what they needed to know for intelligent decision making.
2. In light of their newfound competitive organizational data, they redefined their Mission and developed a different strategic and marketing approach to major markets, pulled out of certain global markets, shrunk their

product line while investing more heavily in a new major product, changed the organizational structure and culture, and acquired a small European company with leading-edge technology.

Within a year, the Greyland division had orchestrated a leveraged buyout, stanched its hemorrhaging, and was meeting its profit objectives. In addition, the company now dominates several of its markets, and its stock has increased in value significantly. In short, the right choice has paid off handsomely.

OPTION ANALYSIS RECONSIDERED

Now let's return to the main character in Chapter 6, Michael Demis, and consider his options from the standpoint of Risk Analysis. As you recall, the management team decided that the best option was to transfer the Wholesale Credit function to the Strategic Business Units in order to concentrate exclusively on the Retail side of the business. What wasn't mentioned in Chapter 6 was the fact that over several days, task teams also did Risk Analyses of their entire plan, probing for what could go wrong, assessing the severity and likelihood of each pitfall, and then planning preventive actions against the Likely Causes, as well as protective actions to minimize the adverse consequences if any of the potential roadblocks did indeed occur. Following is a sampling of their Risk Analyses.

What Could Go Wrong with the Plan?
(High-Priority Potential Risks—18 in total)

1. Attitudes and morale may deteriorate.
   Likely Causes: a. Rumors.
                   b. Poor communication.
2. There could be a letdown in collection efforts.
   Likely Causes: a. Low morale.
                   b. Lack of understanding.

3. If we don't present the Retail acquisition package the right way, and put too many strings on it, our dealers may not buy into and support the decision.
   Likely Causes: a. Presenting it the wrong way.
   b. Dealers may feel hampered by it.
4. We may not be able to maintain the status quo.
5. We may not make the necessary profit.
   Likely Causes (for 4 and 5):
   a. Low morale.
   b. Employees may lean back on the oars.
   c. Employees may become distracted.
6. The three Strategic Business Units may not agree to financing noncompany products.
7. We may lack the necessary resources to implement what we have committed to here.
8. The atmosphere could become more politicized (playing politics).
   Likely Causes (for 6, 7, and 8):
   a. Concern for job security.
   b. Time delay or people left hanging.
   c. Exploring the specific direction without the reasoning behind it.

Examples of preventive action against the occurrence of many of the preceding likely causes (especially numbers 1, 2, and 8) were identified as:

1. We must communicate that there is an Action Calendar developed, especially regarding the Wholesale transfer issue.
2. We need to explain to our people that we have worked through over 200 issues within the past week and a half, and that we have Action Plans relating to most of them but there are still some left that need to be tackled.
3. We must "sell" in a positive manner the Why's, the What's and the How's of these decisions.

4. The sooner we can define the new post-Wholesale organization structure, grade levels, and pay levels, the better.

Preventive actions that counter the Likely Cause of poor direction or misdirection from the top (e.g., in closing offices) include:

1. Issue general ongoing statements about what has been done in terms of implementing the Action Plans.
2. Encourage people to raise questions if they don't understand something.
3. Let senior management know, through upward communication, what people's concerns are, whether or not they have been taken care of by the direct manager.

The Risk Analysis at Demis's company was rigorously applied by the management team. Results of the participants' deliberations were integrated into a master Risk Profile, which, in turn, was used to refine the Communication and Implementation Plan. Small wonder the transition was accomplished so smoothly, and that both Wholesale and Retail volume increased significantly by the end of the first 12 months following execution. The investment of management teamwork in Risk Analysis paid off in millions of dollars of new accounts—many at the expense of the competition ($10 million in the first 4 months and $50 million in incremental sales in the first year)!

CHAPTER ELEVEN

Risk Analysis in Action—2: Responding to World Market Changes

Charles Harner, the new CEO of Spinwell International, a large electronics maker, feared that the lack of a well-thought-out strategic growth plan would increasingly take its toll on the company. The onslaught of Pacific Rim and European competitors in the 1980s painfully drove this point home. Increasingly, Spinwell was becoming less and less a major player in the changing global marketplace: Its pricing was becoming less competitive, and it no longer had a lead role as an innovator in the industry. To add to Spinwell's problems, the company's multilayered organizational structure made it difficult to quickly take advantage of business opportunities.

What kind of strategic changes should Spinwell make to regain its position as a market leader? This is the very question that Harner often asked himself. Although the company certainly had its problems, it did have some significant strategic strengths. Its product designs, though not cutting edge, were of high quality and could be adapted easily to become state-of-the-art and meet changing market requirements. The company also had multiple products and a multidivisional field sales force present in most major markets. And its manufacturing facilities in Canada, Mexico, and the Netherlands, coupled with the basic knowledge to deal with major international markets, did indeed make Spinwell a potential major force in the market.

The key problem was that Spinwell simply had not reacted fast enough to changes in world markets for electronic components. Therefore, the board of directors agreed that Spinwell's senior management team should determine the best way for Spinwell to synchronize itself with the changing currents in the global marketplace.

As you can see from looking at the decision matrix shown in Table 11.1, Spinwell's management, under Harner's guidance, did a thorough job in both establishing and valuing the criteria and in evaluating the options against the criteria. If, however, you examine the management team's Absolute Requirements, you'll see there are no real minimums. This actually makes the criteria more difficult to work with when trying to evaluate each option because so much is left up to subjective judgment. The team also could have done a better job putting an absolute ceiling on the amount of resources they could commit.

You will probably come across situations where it may be very hard for you to place restrictions on your Absolute Requirements. Sure, it's difficult to look into a future that has not yet been written and have to judge if a certain option will indeed meet specific criteria. Just be sure to use as much relevant information as possible, applying to it your own—as well others'—best experience, knowledge, and intuition.

Finally, you will also notice that the management team did a very good job in terms of capturing and writing down information about how well the options met particular Desirable Objectives and then scoring the options accordingly, by reflecting their judgments in a ratio 10-high scale.

As you see from the matrix, there is no clear-cut winner!

Option A does the best job of meeting the criteria, but it is not statistically superior by 15 percent to Option D or even B. Option A, "Organize and provide resources to achieve cost-competitive structure" (with 753 total points), is only 9 percent better than Option D, "Provide project/system engineering capability to serve customer needs" (with 702 points). And Option B, "Structure sales for improved control and penetration of key markets" (682 points), still falls well within the 15 percent guideline range.

Since this was a global strategic decision with enormous impact on the future of the corporation, Harner's team performed a Risk Analysis on all three options. Based on the serious consequences of the decision, the group also decided to conduct a Risk Analysis of Option E, "Cooperate with international firms for joint venture or joint manufacturing."

All of these options are really possible strategies for effectively reacting to the major changes in the global market. They are really How's—"How can we effectively react to major changes in our global market?" You, too, will run across situations much like this where your options really constitute objectives or strategies to reach your ultimate goal and your Decision Purpose.

So Harner's group performed Risk Analyses on the following four options:

A. Organize an integrated design group to permit products and services to be furnished on a competitive basis worldwide.

D. Provide product management and systems engineering capability to better serve customer needs.

B. Structure sales for improved control and penetration of key markets.

E. Assign responsibility, establish procedures, and pursue cooperation with international firms on a joint venture or joint manufacturing basis to increase participation in world markets.

Table 11.1 Key Issue: "We have not reacted effectively to changes in world markets for our machinery"

Decision Purpose: Determine the best way for us to effectively react to changes in the world market

Criteria		Option A			Option B			Option C		
		Organize and provide resources to achieve cost-competitive structure			Structure sales for improved control and penetration of key markets			Establish or buy parts repair facility for non company equipment		

Absolute Requirements

Criteria		Option A			Option B			Option C		
a. Must maintain parts, repair, and service as income base		✓			✓			✓		
b.		✓			✓			✓		
c.		✓			✓			✓		
d.		✓			✓			✓		

Desirable Objectives	V		R	RxV		R	RxV		R	RxV
e. Ensure complete coordination between Machinery Division and Field Services	10	Will help focus	8	80	Will be able to be responsive	9	90	Marginal impact	1	10
f. Achieve more competitive price performance delivery	10	Major impact beneficial	10	100	Improve competitive feedback	4	40	Can quote lower prices on wider customer base	2	20
g. Increase revamp/ retrofit sales in all markets	9	Enlarge number of potential customers or increase profit with same	10	90	Will focus on the market	9	81	Closer to customer. More business other than us	4	36
h. Avoid erosion in share of traditional markets	9	Make us more competitive	9	81	Greater control of business opportunity	6	54	Broaden market base exposure	4	36
i. Increase parts repair and service	9	Help in obtaining market	8	72	Will focus on the market	9	81	Broaden customer base	10	90
j. Achieve measurable penetration of U.S. domestic market in range	8	Ensure greater success probability	10	80	Concentration of effort on key customers	9	72	Increase customer base	2	16
k.										
l.										
m.										
n.										
Total				753			682			249
Rank				1			3			

186

Table 11.1 *(Continued)*

Option D	Option E	Option F	Option G
Provide project/system engineering capability to serve customer needs	Cooperate with international firms for joint venture or joint manufacturing	Use of competitive quality offshore suppliers	Make parts, repair, and service a separate division
✓	✓	✓	✓
✓ ✓ ✓	✓ ✓ ✓	✓	✓ ✓ ✓

	R	RxV		R	RxV		R	RxV		R	RxV
Will have single point entry	10	100	Additional mechanism control market	6	60				Free up product division to focus on next unit effort	6	60
Better control of package installation	7	70	May reduct cost, increase offering technical access	9	90				Will make it more difficult for product division	6	60
Improve effectiveness with customers	9	81	Could provide quicker turnaround	6	54				Greater focus	8	72
Can offer more complete product	8	72	Increase market opportunity	9	81				Increase customer service	6	54
Marginal impact	1	9	Could increase profit level, but possible loss of control	3	27				Focused organization	10	90
More effective package	8	64	May reduce cost, increase offering technical access	2	16				Increase customer base	2	16
	702 2			545			0			386	

187

Tables 11.2-11.5 show Spinwell's Risk Analysis of each of the preceding options. Note that this group did not separate protective action from preventive action in its first cut of Risk Analysis. This was because, in effect, they were Troubleshooting (Step 7 of the Option Analysis Process) their four best options rather than homing in on a (tentatively) chosen one. But not doing so resulted, as you'll see, in a number of "shotgun" actions, that is, broader, more time-consuming and expensive actions that might have not been necessary had they analyzed for more specific Likely Causes.

You've probably noticed that there is a lot of risk to Recommendation A, Table 11.2, requiring very careful analysis and planning to make it work. The actions in the last column represent the team's initial thinking. When the team members actually chose to execute the option, they had to develop a specific program to accomplish each of the actions since six of the seven risks were assessed as "High Impact" and any one of them could have proven very damaging.

With regard to Recommendation D, Table 11.3, and with the exception of Risk a, the team assessed this option as having moderate to relatively low risk. Note that the managers decided not to develop actions relative to Risks d and e for this reason. They did feel that certain specified actions would avoid Risks c and b.

Note that the actions designated against Risks b and f of Recommendation B, Table 11.4, are not preventive, but rather are protective. That is, they don't reduce the likelihood of either problem happening, but simply are stated in terms of "What to do in case of . . ."

Even though the original Option E, "Cooperate with international firms for joint venture or joint manufacturing," fell out more than 25 percent behind the leading Option A, it initially had been favored by two senior managers in the group. Because they were nonplused that it fared so poorly (their "gut feel" suggested that something was wrong with the analysis,

Table 11.2 Risk Analysis of Recommendation A: Organize an integrated design group to permit products and services to be furnished on a competitive basis worldwide

Potential Risks	Impact	Chance	Preventive or Protective Action
a. Sacred cows.	H	H	Top management makes clear that there are *no* sacred cows; any subject is open for discussion.
b. We may not have sufficient people or resource mix.	H	M	Carefully assess needs and make certain the plan is developed to ensure people and other resources are available when needed.
c. Our organization may not have flexibility to adapt.	H	H	Structure requires close attention and careful selection of key staff members against specific criteria.
d. Competitive cost levels may not be achieved.	H	H	Organize to procure from all sourcing areas. Need to have audit procedures established, to be certain all disciplines respond to the necessity.
e. Our resources may not be correctly applied (i.e., some may be applied to "non"-markets.).	M	M	Survey market, evaluate results, and assign priorities for ongoing product cost reduction.
f. Assumptions may be made about products and services without testing true market demand.	H	MH	Test market demand by selected internal and external sources.
g. People may have "not invented here" (NIH) attitude.	H	M	Ensure personnel are carefully selected and trained to understand need for selected competitive products and services.

Table 11.3 Risk Analysis of Recommendation D: Provide project management and systems engineering capability to better serve customer needs

Potential Risks	Impact	Chance	Preventive and Protective Action
a. We may not have the talent.	H	H	Define talents needed, carefully screen incumbents, and develop or hire. Cooperate as appropriate with noncompetitive vendors through subcontracting basis.
b. Our division may not be structured to accomplish it.	H	M	Restructure specific organizational units.
c. The company may not accept the risk.	M	M	*Policy* must be established *beforehand* as to acceptable scope, so that there is no doubt which projects will be pursued.
d. We may possibly alienate traditional clients in the U.S. market.	L	L	
e. Doing this may not be as necessary as we believe.	L	L	

although they could not find fault with the judgments made), the CEO suggested that a Risk Analysis be done of it also. The results are shown in Table 11.5.

Although many readers, based on their own experience, might speculate that this joint venture partner option might be fraught with potential pitfalls—and indeed it did not fare well in the Option Analysis—the management team believed that, with the exceptions of e and h, this was a relatively low-risk option.

Table 11.4 Risk Analysis of Recommendation B: Structure sales for improved control and penetration of key markets

Potential Risks	Impact	Chance	Preventive and Protective Action
a. People may be in wrong place.	H	H	Must assign people on the basis of who is right for a particular market.
b. We may have the wrong people.	H	M	Terminate or reassign.
c. Our people may have inadequate training.	M	L	
d. Responsibilities may not be sufficiently defined.	M	M	
e. Some key people not flexible to move?	H	M	Analyze and plan both preventive and protective actions.
f. Salespeople may be ineffective.	H	H	Terminate or reassign.
g. People may not be properly compensated.	M	M	

Based on the preceding analysis, the management group recommended—and CEO Harner approved—an Implementation Plan for some of the following Key Plan Elements:

1. Organize an integrated machinery group to permit products and services to be furnished on a competitive basis in selected global areas, while withdrawing from others. [Option A]
   a. Establish a coordinated global marketing organization that reports to the manager of the design group.

Table 11.5 Risk Analysis of Recommendation E:
Assign responsibility, establish procedures,
and pursue cooperation with international firms on
joint venture or joint manufacturing basis
to increase participation in world markets

Potential Risks	Impact	Chance	Preventive and Protective Action
a. We could lose technology, design, and manufacturing.	L	L	Control "hot" parts.
b. We could develop a competitor.	M	L	License hardware, not background technology. Carefully draw up contract with built-in controls, and assign/police responsibility with adequate resources. Control "hot" parts.
c. This could be costly. All efforts to support joint venture partners could be detrimental to our own business.	M	H	Must carefully assess beforehand and provide contractual opportunities for renegotiation.
d. The situation could be difficult to control.	M	H	Assign individual to be resident on site and work closely to monitor the status of the activities and results.
e. We are not currently organized to support this.	H	H	Organize effort and establish standards to ensure quality product is supplied. Get experienced people involved to avoid pitfalls.
f. We might have possible language and communication problems.	M	M	Hire multilingual people.
g. We could have possible currency problems.	M	M	Provide "hedging."
h. Contracts could be poorly drawn, allowing partners to go off on their own	H	M	Use best technical, commercial, and legal expertise to assist in developing the contract; have sufficient legal staff.

  b. Establish the project management concept in a major division with a specific organizational realignment. [Option D]

2. Structure sales for control and penetration of key markets. [Option B]
   a. Define the products.
   b. Identify customers most likely to buy those products and services over the next 3 years.
   c. Determine which global markets and areas to withdraw from.
   d. Determine which products to prune and how best to do so.
   e. Analyze existing offices and staff to determine the most effective utilization and restructuring.
   f. Review field salespeople's effectiveness and skills for staffing and upgrading.

The whole plan was further specified in terms of *what* had to be accomplished, *by when*, and *who* had major authority and accountability. Lower levels of management were then briefed in detail on the plan; it appeared so well thought through that they gave their buy-in once they understood the "Why's" and "Wherefore's." Functioning as a "wired-together" team, the managers fleshed out their portions of the plan—and effectively implemented it. Today, Spinwell has regained its market share and appears to be well on its way to becoming a world-class competitor in its field.

What about Option E? In view of the resources—time, people, and so forth—that Spinwell would have to apply to implement the three options selected, the team felt that also trying to achieve the fourth, low-risk option would strain the organization too much. Therefore, Option E was rejected.

PART IV

The Complete
Thought Process

CHAPTER TWELVE

The Complete Thought Process

Your alarm clock malfunctioned and you're late for work. . . . Your car won't start. . . . You finally get to the office and learn that all of a sudden a manufacturing process that's worked flawlessly for 20 years is now spitting out undeliverable product. . . . There's a computer crisis on the third floor. . . . In the afternoon, a competitor announces a breakthrough product, this on the heels of a front-page article that pans your new release. . . . There's talk of a strike. . . . And on your way to an emergency strategy session that will last through dinner and into the wee hours, you realize that you forgot your wedding anniversary. . . .

Of course, few of us have this many problems—big and small—in a single day. But the small problems continue to plague us, and the big problems, though perhaps sporadic, are inevitable hurdles that will materialize over the weeks and months. You can either take them as they come, in a "firefighting" mode, or you can learn to instantly react by using the tools of the *Complete Thought Process* (Root Cause Analysis, Option Analysis, and Risk/Opportunity Analysis). This chapter reviews each component and shows you how to quickly use all three, so you can approach any problem from "cradle to grave" by finding the cause, selecting your options, and determining what can derail your efforts before you take action.

In the following pages you'll find:

- Process questions that will help solidify your understanding of the three types of analyses.
- An opportunity to solve a "management whodunit" concerning an airline, and to assess what's wrong with an Option Analysis performed by a manufacturing operation.
- Key issues regarding the implementation of the three methodologies.
- Guidance for investing time and energy when applying the *Complete Thought Process.*
- Advice on how to make decisions under tight time constraints, and crystallize the best thinking and buy-in from Option Analysis.

ROOT CAUSE PROCESS QUESTIONS

Try answering these questions on your own. Then turn to the next section and compare your answers with the recommended approach.

1. Should you test the "distinctions" you've developed against the description of what the "Crime (problem) is" and "Crime is not"?
2. What is the question you should ask when destructively testing for the most probable cause?
3. How should you state your Problem Definition when analyzing for Root Cause?
4. To what should you keep relating the description of "the Crime" in Root Cause Analysis?
5. How should you handle the persistent obstructionist in any group while systematically trying to find the cause of a problem?
6. What questions should you ask to help distinguish and *prioritize* the most important issues from the others?

7. Where should your experience come into play in the Root Cause Analysis process?
8. What questions should you ask to develop distinctions?
9. How should you develop hypotheses as to what may be the most probable cause of a problem or opportunity?
10. What should the process be for finding the root cause of an opportunity—something that's gone *better* than expected?

Answers to Root Cause Questions

1. *Should you test the "distinctions" you've developed against the description of what the "Crime (problem) is" and "Crime is not"?*

No. There is no need to test the "distinctions" against the description of what the "Crime is" versus what it is not. Instead, you should test your diagnosis (i.e., hypotheses) about probable causes—and any other causes people have raised as suspect—in terms of the description of what the Crime is and what it is *not*. Remember, distinctions are the "bridge" to lead you from these two descriptions to what may be the most probable cause(s), which you then in turn can test against your description.

2. *What is the question you should ask when destructively testing for the most probable cause?*

The most helpful question you can ask when destructively testing any possible or probable cause is: "If 'X' is the most probable cause, then why does the problem exist *here* of this exact *nature* at this particular *time* and in this scope (in the "is" description) and not there (i.e., the identity, location, and time of the "is not" description)? To destructively test, try to "shoot down" any and all possible causes. Do *not* try to build up, explain, or justify what you think may be the most probable cause.

3. *How should you state your Problem Definition when analyzing for Root Cause?*

When stating your Problem Definition, use the "FOG" approach (i.e., a statement that is Factual, Observable, and General). The more simple the statement, the better it is for starting off your Root Cause Analysis: This way, you don't risk building any assumed causes into your definition of the Crime that could lead you to a wrong conclusion.

4. *To what should you keep relating the description of "the Crime" in Root Cause Analysis?*

Keep asking the three specifying questions of *identity, location,* and *time* (with the scope of each) of your Problem Definition. This will help you focus your description on the object for which you're really trying to find Cause. Doing this may help you realize that, based on your description, you have strayed from the definition and are describing some other problem or condition— and you may recognize the need to change your Problem Definition accordingly.

5. *How should you handle the persistent obstructionist in any group while systematically trying to find the cause of the problem?*

There are many ways to handle such people who resist this discipline and approach to keeping on track. For example, ask why they feel a certain way, and what data they have to make such an opinion. Test their data against what you've already learned about the Crime— i.e., its definition, description (Can you shoot it down yet?), and distinctions, or a probable cause drawn from the distinctions. Despite their persistence, objectionists rarely have data to short-circuit the process. In fact,

200

obstructionists often have hidden agendas, and this is one way to flush them out. Also, if you're in a group, you may ask what everyone thinks about what the obstructionist has said, and if they agree or disagree. By keeping to the sequential process and asking process-focused questions, you should be able to tactfully help the obstructionist understand "where in the sequence" he or she is, versus where he or she *should be.*

6. *What questions should you ask to help distinguish and* prioritize *the most important Issues from the others?*
   When you prioritize the most important issues, you should do so in terms of their probable impact, urgency, and growth trend, and the amount of information that seems readily available.

7. *Where should your experience come into play in the Root Cause Analysis process?*
   Your experience and intuition can help you know where to look for and how to ask for information to define and describe the Crime. Just be sure you're working with factual data and not assumptions or wishful thinking. In the Description Phase, you want "just the facts," or no less than reasonable inferences—and no assumptions. Flag (place an asterisk by) any information that you suspect as possibly not reliable. In the Distinguishing Phase—and based on your experience, gut, and intuition—certain discrepancies should stand out as unique, peculiar, or different when you compare what the "Crime (problem) is" with what the "Crime is not."

8. *What questions should you ask to develop distinctions?*
   The questions you should ask to develop distinctions are: "What is peculiar? What is different? What is unique?" to the description of the Crime (problem) in

contrast to the description of what the Crime is not in terms of *identity, location,* and *time.* If there are several elements of the "Crime is" dimensions, then ask, "What do these have in common in contrast to what's *not* the what, where, when (and scope) of the Crime?"

9. *How should you develop hypotheses as to what may be the most probable cause of a problem or opportunity?*
Of each distinction ask, "How could this factor that is unique or peculiar to the 'Crime is,' as distinct from the 'Crime is not,' have caused this problem or opportunity? Are there any reasonable hypotheses?" If so, list them and, when you destructively test each, try to shoot them down on the basis of the information on both sides of the Crime dimension.

10. *What should the process be for finding the root cause of an opportunity—something that's gone* better *than expected?*
Use the identical process.

There can be a real payoff to finding and verifying the cause of an opportunity; if it doesn't have significant undesirable consequences, you may determine how to keep it happening and getting positive results for you—you may even be able to use it to cause similar results in other facets of your business or home life.

Root Cause Review

Here are the key questions to ask in order to take each of the seven steps:

1. *Prioritize*
   - What has the highest impact (consequences/payoff)?
   - What is the most urgent and pressing?
   - Is the problem apt to grow considerably if not solved soon?

- Does it appear that you have access to sufficient information to at least begin the analysis?

2. *Define the problem*
   - What's happening that shouldn't be, and what's *not* happening that should be?
   - What is going especially well—so well that you'd like to find its cause?
   - F.O.G.—State it at a Factual, Observable, and General level.
   - Do you know why you have this problem or opportunity? How do you know? How did you verify it?

3. *Description*
   - Ask specifying questions to describe the *What* (identity), *Where* (location), and *When* (timing) of your concern. Flip the question over to find out *What, Where,* and *When* it's not happening and is not of concern.
   - What is the scope or magnitude of each dimension?
   - What are the calendar and clock time? Is there any periodicity?
   - Test yourself: Ask why you are asking a particular question or writing a piece of information into the *identity, location,* or *time* boxes of your description (i.e., does this information attempt to answer the question "Why?" or "What, Where, When?"—and how many or how much of each? If it is an attempt to answer the question "Why?" then you risk building in an assumed cause. (This happens so easily!) If so, take it out!

4. *Differentiate/distinguish*
   - What is peculiar, odd, unique, or distinctive to the "Crime (problem) is" happening as opposed to What, Where, and When the "Crime is not" happening? What do elements of the Crime have in *common* as distinct from their opposites that are *not* part of the Crime?

- What has the sharpest contrast between What, Where, and When the "Crime is" and What, Where, and When the "Crime is not"?

5. *Diagnose for most probable cause*
   - What is it about each distinction that could have caused this particular problem or opportunity in the dimensions and respects you've identified?

6. *Destructively test*
   - Do you have enough good, accurate, descriptive data about the Crime (or opportunity) in the Is/Is not columns for use in testing and trying to destroy possible causes?
   - If this hypothesis is the cause of this specific problem or opportunity as dimensioned, why is it only the characteristics of the Crime's identity, location, and time—and scope of each—that are involved, and not what, when, and where the Crime is *not* (including how many, how much, etc.).
   - What assumptions do you have to make outside the Crime is/is not data for this distinction to remain as a probable cause? Can you find information to validate the hypothesis in these respects?
   - Is additional information needed to test further?
   - If you've shot down all probable causes, is there apt to be invalid data in the Crime is/is not dimension?
   - Is there another possible hypothesis from one or two distinctions? Are there apt to be more distinctions? What piece(s) of data shot down most hypotheses?
   - How can you empirically verify that this indeed is *the* Cause?

7. *Decide*
   - What *corrective* action can you take to eliminate the cause?

- What *preventive* action can you take to avoid or remove likely causes in the future from creating the same or similar problems?
- What *opportunistic* action can you take to keep the cause in effect and capitalize on the unexpected opportunity?

Now apply these questions to the following actual problem that a U.S. airline recently experienced. See if you can solve this "management whodunit." (The scenario is adapted from an actual case.)

IN-FLIGHT FEVER

Crosswinds Air Lines has grown by leaps and bounds, with a superior safety record. Recently, however, about 90 flight attendants reported approximately 150 instances of red spots on their skin, mostly during the past 2 months. What baffled the doctors was the strange pattern of the condition, which didn't affect passengers or pilots. Curiously, more than 90 percent of the cases occurred on the A300, the new European Airbus that Crosswinds had just purchased for use in the United States. A few cases were reported on the L-1011 and 727 jets. Oddly, the cases didn't occur on A300 overland routes—only on routes that went over the water. Yet no reports of the problem were filed by attendants on Crosswinds DC-9s that flew over water.

Some flight attendants who developed the red spots reported burning and itching on their faces, and some feared their appearance might be harmed. In fact, several attendants reported severe burning that lasted for days. As you can well imagine, the report of the cases found its way into the media, which caused a 30 percent drop in ticket sales on Crosswinds flights.

It's up to you to get to the most probable cause and recommend corrective action, before the airline faces severe financial difficulties and a permanently tarnished reputation! Use the analysis capture sheet (Table 12.1) for your work.

Table 12.1 Executrak® Success or Failure Analysis Capture Sheet

DEFINE: What's different from what you expected? (What's happening that *shouldn't* be? What isn't happening that *should* be?)

DESCRIBE: Magnitude in terms of:

	Crime Is	Crime Is Not
Identity (What)	S	
	C	
Location (Where)	O	
	P	
Time (When)	E	

DISTINGUISH: What is different, peculiar, or unique to the Crime in contrast with what the Crime is not, especially where you see *sharp* contrasts?

DIAGNOSE: Most likely cause(s):

DESTRUCTIVELY TEST: To determine whether one or more hypotheses about a distinguishing factor *cannot* be "shot down" by your test as the Most Probable Cause:

"If *(X)* is the cause of *(Y)*, why is it only (Crime is)?
Why isn't it (Crime is not)?"

MOST PROBABLE CAUSE IS:
(The Option Analysis Process can help in deciding the best way to extinguish the problem permanently.)

Although you may not have any data to pinpoint the most probable causes, as a good management "whodunit" sleuth, you should have a very specific description of the Crime is/is not dimension from which you can draw possible distinctions. At worst, you should know exactly what you're looking for as the most probable cause.

(A second capture sheet [Table 12.2] has been filled in with the actual data against which you can compare your answers. Don't look at it until you have completed your own analysis.)

Solving the Crosswinds Mystery

Time-consuming empirical testing of all sorts finally led to the discovery that the red ink flaking came primarily from new vests with especially thick lettering. The new vests were placed on Crosswinds's newest planes, the A300s, explaining why most cases occurred on those planes. Some new vests, however, were placed on L-1011 and 727 jets, causing a few cases on those planes. There weren't any incidents on the Crosswinds DC-9 fleet, since the DC-9 uses seat cushions as flotation devices in case a plane has to land on water. Crosswinds found that the ink was indeed the culprit, which was confirmed by tests conducted by the U.S. Center for Disease Control in Atlanta.

Having cracked this difficult "whodunit" with Root Cause Analysis, let's consider the second step of the Complete Thought Process—Option Analysis. Knowing the answers to the following questions will help you quickly find the best option once you've identified the Root Cause. (The recommended answers are provided on the following pages.)

Table 12.2   Executrak® Success or Failure Analysis Capture Sheet

DEFINE: What's different from what you expected? (What's happening that *shouldn't* be? What isn't happening that *should* be?) <u>There are red spots appearing on skin that shouldn't be there.</u>

DESCRIBE: Magnitude in terms of:

		Crime Is	Crime Is Not
Identity (What)	**S**	Tiny red spots on the skin. Reddish-colored perspiration. Some reports of burning and itching.	Sores, skin abrasions, or lacerations. Large spots, other coloration. High incidence of burning and itching.
	C		
Location (Where)		More than 90% on new A300 European Airbus, a few on both the L-1011	All A300 flights, DC-9 over-water routes, most L-1011 or 727 jets.
	O	and 727 jets. 90 flight attendants, 150 instances. Mainly flights over water.	Passengers or pilots, or all flight attendants. Mainly overland flights.
	P	Face, head, and neck area.	Any other part of the body.
Time (When)	**E**	Within the past 2 months.	Before.

DISTINGUISH: What is different, peculiar, or unique to the Crime in contrast with what the Crime is not, especially where you see *sharp* contrasts?
   <u>There is something relatively new; these attendants are wearing or using something, or standing somewhere that is affecting only their face, head, and neck.</u>

DIAGNOSE: Most likely cause(s): <u>Attendants performing demonstrations with life vests; so it may be something about the life vests causing redness; *i.e.*, lettering, contaminants, etc.</u>

DESTRUCTIVELY TEST: To determine whether one or more hypotheses about a distinguishing factor *cannot* be "shot down" by your test as the Most Probable Cause. (Test against Description.)

"If *life jacket lettering (X)* causes *red spots (Y)*,
                    why is it only *face, head, and neck*? (Crime Is)
                    Why isn't it *other parts of body*? (Crime Is Not)

MOST PROBABLE CAUSE IS: Check life vests around neck area for thick coloring or contaminants. (Use the Option Analysis Process to decide on the best way(s) to extinguish the problem *permanently*.)

OPTION ANALYSIS PROCESS QUESTIONS

1. What is the potential pitfall if you do not sufficiently define the criteria and options before you evaluate them?
2. What constitutes an "Absolute Requirement" (i.e., what are its requirements)?
3. Should you write down the information defining the Desirable Objectives before weighing them?
4. How should you evaluate options against the criteria? What are the key questions?

Answers to Option Analysis Questions

1. *What is the potential pitfall if you do not sufficiently define the criteria and options before you evaluate them?*

   If you do not define the criteria and options sufficiently before you evaluate them, there may be areas of misperception or confusion about what that particular criterion or option really means. This will make it more difficult to be sure that you'll make the best decision for its purpose, nor will you be readily able to evaluate the criterion in terms of whether it is an Absolute Requirement, a Desirable Objective, or an option.

2. *What constitutes an Absolute Requirement (i.e., what are its requirements)?*

   An Absolute Requirement must not only be considered *absolutely essential*; it also must have an absolute minimum level of acceptable performance (Result) or cost less than a maximum amount of time, money, or other resource you have available. There must also be some form of measurement—some ceiling or limit placed on the Absolute Requirement—or else it will not function for you in reality as a true "Absolute Requirement."

   Absolute Requirements that do not have absolutely essential minimum or maximum parameters will make it harder for you and others to evaluate the alternatives to determine which truly will or should meet the requirement and which won't. The more fuzzily the requirement is stated, the more subjectivity creeps in and the more argumentation is likely to ensue. This makes evaluation a difficult task.

3. *Should you write down the information defining the Desirable Objectives before weighing them?*
You don't necessarily have to put down the information defining Desirable Objectives criteria before weighing them if there are only a few and it is a relatively simple decision. If, however, the analysis is complex with a number of criteria, and if it will involve many people, then it may indeed help to make explicit the information about each criterion.

4. *How should you evaluate options against the criteria? What are the key questions?*
There are two ways to evaluate the options against the criteria. When evaluating each option against the Absolute Requirements, take one option at a time and assess it against each and every Absolute Requirement, asking: "Does this option meet the first Absolute Requirement? What information leads me to believe this?" If it meets it, then go on to evaluate it against the next, and so forth.

When evaluating the options against the Desirable Objectives, assess across the options "horizontally." Looking at the first criterion, ask: "Which option does the best job of meeting this one criterion, and why?" After putting down the information of why that option does the best job, give it a value of 10 (writing it in the matrix box), and then ask the following question: "Which of the remaining options does the *next* best job of meeting this criterion? Why?" and write down the data supporting this judgment in the matrix box. Then score it in terms of how many points you would give it in relation to the 10-scored option. Is it 50 percent as good? Then give it a 5. Is it 90 percent? Give it a 9, and so on. After you've filled in all the boxes under the options for that one criterion, proceed on to your next criterion, assessing the options the same way.

In an even more rigorous analysis, to help reduce the likelihood of bias creeping into judgments, "smoke out" *all* the relevant information on *all* the options for one or more criteria *before* retracing your steps and evaluating them on the basis of that data, only then scoring the options accordingly. This method is superior to the former, though a bit more time-consuming because the sooner you start reflecting your judgments in terms of numbers without comparative data on all the options, the more risk there is to losing objectivity.

Following are the key questions to further strengthen your Option Analysis:

Option Analysis Review

1. *Smoke out the issues*
   - Why is any decision necessary—what would be the serious consequences if you didn't tackle the issue now?
   - What are the issues surrounding this decision?
   - Is Option Analysis the right management tool to use? Do you first need to find the cause for the key issue before trying to determine what to do about it?
   - List the issues before trying to evaluate or debate them.
   - Prioritize: What is the most important issue to tackle first?

2. *Define the decision purpose*
   - What really needs to be determined?
   - "Why do you want to determine this?"
   - State it in non-binary (i.e., not either/or, yes/no) terms.

3. *Establish criteria*
   - What are you trying to *achieve, preserve,* and *avoid* as problems by whatever you decide?
   - Do the issues you've already developed suggest any other criteria?
   - What are the parameters or specifications you are trying to meet by this decision?
   - Can you eliminate duplication and consolidate any criteria?
   - Can you flip the coin over, "translating" any negatives (Avoids) into positives (i.e., what you really want to Achieve)?

4. *Prioritize criteria*
   - First "rough cut"—High/Medium/Low.
   - Are any of the "Highs" *absolutely essential* to meet without fail?
   - If so, what are the "measurables" ("deliverables with metrics"), the *minimum* acceptable level of performance required for any option to be worthy of further consideration, or *maximum* amount of time, money, or other resources that can be expended?
   - Are there any Absolute Requirements that should also be reflected as Desirable Objectives to give further credit to any options that exceed the absolute minimum required performance or will cost less than the maximum of that type of resource?
   - What are the other Desirable Objectives?
   - How will you reflect the relative performance of these objectives (i.e., a 10-high ratio scale?)

5. *Identify possible options*
   - What are various ways to meet your criteria/priorities?
   - Think about different scenarios/strategies/possible solutions.
   - Use "focused brainstorming" by creating options from

each criterion (i.e., looking for "Hows" or "Ways" to meet each one).

- Check back to Step 1 (issues) for additional ideas on options.

6. *Evaluate options against criteria*
   - Set up in matrix format.
   - Balance "gut feel" with logic and information.
   - Evaluate the options based on data and information.
   - Write down information first, then reflect your best judgment in relative numbers (ratios).
   - Does each option meet every single Absolute Requirement? If not, "shoot it down"! Get rid of it! Or you'll risk ending up selecting an option that fails to satisfy what you've determined is really essential to Achieve, Preserve, or Avoid.
   - Which of the remaining options does the best job of meeting the Desirable Objectives?
   - Is it 15 percent more or better than any of the other options? Are there any characteristics of the options that did well in these areas, and can be combined with them?
   - If the best option(s) did poorly on one or more highly Desirable Objectives, how can it (or they) be strengthened? Will the resources required to do so be worth it? Once strengthened at whatever additional resource costs, does it score even better against the other options?

7. *Troubleshoot*
   - Take the tentative choice and troubleshoot it (i.e., where is it weak? What could go wrong with it that can't be factored in as criteria? What can be done to reduce such "flat spots"?).
   - Can the "winner" be strengthened?

Table 12.3 is an actual application that has been altered for learning purposes. You do not have to understand the content to be able to figure out what is wrong with the matrix.

Table 12.3 How many process errors or questions can you find?

Line	The Best Way to Insert Leaded Decoupling Capacitors:	Weight	%	OPTION 1: Manual Insertion	R	RxV	OPTION 2: Multi-Head Dip Insertion	R	RxV	OPTION 3: Robotics (Retooled)	R	RxV	OPTION 4: Robotics (New)	R	RxV
2	ABSOLUTES:														
	1) Meet OSHA standards			Yes			Yes			Yes			Yes		
	2) Be capable of .150 grid spacing insertion			Yes			Yes			Yes			Yes		
	3) Be accurate within +/– .005			Yes			Yes			—			—		
	4) Provide capability of .300 lead center lines			Yes			Yes			—			—		
3	DESIRABLES:														
	Meet DOD 2000 & 6536:	10	10%		1	10		10	100		10	100		10	100
	- Ability to clench leads			Yes			Yes			Yes			Yes		
	- Meet ESD requirements			Yes Handle parts			Yes			Yes			Yes		
	- View the point after solder			Yes			Yes			Yes			Yes		
4	Be reliable	9	9%		7	63		9.5	85.5		9	81		9	81
5	Provide for positive insertion without prior preparation	9	9%	Human insertion	7	63	Grabs leads; inserts at proper angle	10	90	Fore-sensing combs leads	10	90	Fore-sensing combs leads	10	90

214

#	Criterion	Imp.	%	Concept 1			Concept 2			Concept 3			Concept 4		
6	Minimize set-up time	8	8%	60 minutes clean mach.	2.5	20	15 minutes	10	80	15 minutes load fixture, load parts, program	10	80	15 minutes	10	80
7	Maximize rate of insertion	8	8%	300/hour	1	8	2,700/hour	10	80	1,450/hour	5	40	1,450/hour	5	40
8	Minimize operator attendance	8	8%	constant attention	0	0	25% free time	2.5	20	75% free time	7.5	60	75% free time	7.5	60
9	Be easy to use by the operator	8	8%		0	0		10	80	Menu-driven, CRT intfc, fault isolation	10	80		10	80
10	Provide for CAD interface capability	9	8%	No	0	0	Yes	10	80	Yes	10	80	Yes	10	80
11	Be maintainable	7	7%	No machine maint.	10	70	2 hours/week	5	35	1 hour/week	6	42	1 hour/week	6	42
12	Be a standard/"turnkey" system	7	7%	Yes	10	70	Yes	10	70	Some customization	8	56	Some customization	8	56
13	Maximize ROI	6	6%			0			0			0			0
14	Provide capability of .255 lead center lines	4	4%	Yes	10	40	No	10	40	Yes	10	40	Yes	10	40
15	Be easy to use by the engineer	4	4%		4	16	Menu-driven	8	32	Menu-driven more complex	7	28	Menu-driven more complex	7	28
16	Total	96	100%			360			762.5			777			777
												WINNER			WINNER

215

Errors / Questions about the Analysis

1. No data appears under the options relative to the third and fourth Absolute Requirements. On what basis, therefore, are they all being evaluated against the Desirable Objectives? Is it possible that one or more could have been "shot down" on the Absolute Requirements if the relevant information had been obtained? If so, it would have ensured that one or more options would *not* be unwisely chosen—and certainly have saved the time it took to evaluate against all the Desirable Objectives.

2. No need for a percentage column on Desirable Objectives. A "10-high" scale is sufficient. A percentage scale is more cumbersome.

3. Line 3: Options 2-4 all receive 10's. Are there any real differences between them? If the information was more specific, it might help differentiate judgments that could then be more accurately reflected.

4. The 10 given to the first Desirable Objective should be spread among the three sub-objectives to accurately reflect their relative weights: 5, 3, and 2, for example.

5. Line 4: No data is visible under the Options, nor is the best Option given 10 points. Using a 10-high scale, not only should the most important objective receive 10 points, but the option with the best score on *each* Objective should also receive a 10. (If two or more do equally well, they all should receive 10's. Using a 10-high scale, whatever option does best—even if it's not ideal—should get a 10.)

6. Line 4: Option 2 (as well as later lines and options) has a decimal point. Do not use decimal points. Can you really judge within a 5 percent risk of error? Decimal points really have very little numerical significance and may confuse the issue.

7. Lines 6-10 (Criteria Weights): Are there no differentiations in the relative value of these five Criteria? The more criteria you have valued the same in your best judgment,

the less potential differentiation you will be able to build into your analysis of the options and the more difficult it will be to make a clear decision with confidence.

8. Line 13: Don't any of the options, no matter how seemingly poor, fulfill, to any degree, the criterion of maximizing ROI? Giving all of them 0's can be interpreted to mean they all do a negligible job. "Which one best satisfies this Criterion?" should be the question; the best option should receive 10 points and the others scored downwards accordingly.

9. Line 14: All options are given 10's. Do some score better than others? If so, this should be reflected accordingly.

10. Line 15: Again, Option 2, which is evaluated the best, should be scored 10 and the others "ratio'd down" from the 10 accordingly.

11. Line 16: Option 4 is designated as the "Winner" but is tied with Option 3 and has no statistically significant advantage over Option 2! How can an intelligent choice be made at this point as to which really is the best option?

What should you do in a situation like this? Look for where each scored poorly, especially against highly weighted objectives, and determine what it would cost in relevant resources (i.e., time, money, people, etc.) to strengthen each in these areas. If the benefits outweigh the costs, rescore the options and see what the totals reveal. Most important, do the results of the rescoring make sense? If not, retrace your steps and evaluate your judgments at each of the Seven Step Milestones to determine just what troubles you and what you should decide at that point.

General Comments

1. There is not one criterion for minimizing cost, although it may have been considered as part of Maximize ROI (line 13). But since all four options rated 0 on this, it would be

Table 12.4 Answer Sheet (Note: Errors are highlighted in bold print and underlined.)

Line	The Best Way to Insert Leaded Decoupling Capacitors:	Weight	%	OPTION 1: Manual Insertion			OPTION 2: Multi-Head Dip Insertion			OPTION 3: Robotics (Retooled)			OPTION 4: Robotics (New)		
					R	RxV		R	RxV		R	RxV		R	RxV
1															
2	*ABSOLUTES:*														
	1) Meet OSHA standards			Yes			Yes			Yes			Yes		
	2) Be capable of .150 grid spacing insertion			Yes			Yes			Yes			Yes		
	3) Be accurate within +/- .005			Yes			Yes			—			—		
	4) Provide capability of .300 lead center lines			Yes			Yes			—			—		
3	*DESIRABLES:* Meet DOD 2000 & 6536:	10	**10%**		1	10		**10**	100		**10**	100		**10**	100
	- Ability to clench leads			Yes			Yes			Yes			Yes		
	- Meet ESD requirements			Yes (Handle parts)			Yes			Yes			Yes		
	- View the point after solder			Yes			Yes			Yes			Yes		
4	Be reliable	9	**9%**		7	63		**9.5**	85.5		9	81		9	81
5	Provide for positive insertion without prior preparation	9	**9%**	Human insertion	7	63	Grabs leads; inserts at proper angle	10	90	Fore-sensing combs leads	10	90	Fore-sensing combs leads	10	90

#	Requirement	Wt	%	Alt A value	A	A wt	Alt B value	B	B wt	Alt C value	C	C wt	Alt D value	D	D wt
6	Minimize set-up time	8	8%	60 minutes clean mach.	2.5	20	15 minutes	10	80	15 minutes load fixture, load parts, program	10	80	15 minutes	10	80
7	Maximize rate of insertion	8	8%	300/hour	1	8	2,700/hour	10	80	1,450/hour	5	40	1,450/hour	5	40
8	**Minimize operator attendance**	8	8%	constant attention	0	0	25% free time	2.5	20	75% free time	7.5	60	75% free time	7.5	60
9	**Be easy to use by the operator**	8	8%		0	0		10	80	Menu-driven, CRT intfc, fault isolation	10	80		10	80
10	Provide for CAD interface capability	9	8%	No	0	0	Yes	10	80	Yes	10	80	Yes	10	80
11	Be maintainable	7	7%	No machine maint.	10	70	2 hours/week	5	35	1 hour/week	6	42	1 hour/week	6	42
12	Be a standard/"turnkey" system	7	7%	Yes	10	70	Yes	10	70	Some customization	8	56	Some customization	8	56
13	Maximize ROI	6	6%		0	0		0	0		0	0		0	0
14	Provide capability of .255 lead center lines	4	4%	Yes	10	40	No	10	40	Yes	10	40	Yes	10	40
15	**Be easy to use by the engineer**	4	4%	Menu-driven	4	16	Menu-driven more complex	8	32	Menu-driven more complex	7	28	Menu-driven more complex	7	28
16	Total	96	100%			360			762.5			777			777 WINNER

219

preferable to at least modify the criterion to read "Minimize Cost."

2. Options 3 and 4 scored within 1 point of each other throughout the analysis. Are there any significant differences between the two options? If not, can they be combined?

3. Can the criteria on Lines 8, 9, and 15 be condensed into one criterion without any danger? As it stands, they all deal with the human factor. Together, they total 20 points, twice as many as the most important 10-weighted criterion. Does this really reflect how the managers who performed this analysis feel?

Table 12.4 highlights these problems (in bold print).

OPTION ANALYSIS UNDER TIGHT TIME CONSTRAINTS

It may appear to you that going through the seven-step decision process can be time-consuming or cumbersome. The sequence of steps, however, actually enables you to judge roughly how much time to allocate to each. When you don't have a lot of time to make a decision, or when a decision is not of serious enough consequence to warrant a longer analysis, it's possible to do a "tight time pressure" decision analysis (i.e., in 10 minutes or less).

In other instances, you may find—through Risk Analysis Troubleshooting (Step 7)—that insufficient time was given to a decision and enough significant concerns are raised that it makes sense to back up and invest more time analyzing it.

To practice "tight time pressure" decision making, pick a decision that is not of severe consequence to you (for example, where to eat dinner Saturday night, what to wear for a business luncheon, the best "grab-bag" gift to buy, how to spend a day off from work, etc.).

You'll notice from the following list that the only step not present is "Smoking out the issues." This is because, with so little time to complete your analysis, the time investment would not be worth the effort.

So, if you have selected an issue, invest 10 minutes in the following manner and see how you would evaluate your ROI (return on investment).

30 seconds—Decision *purpose.*
2 minutes—Establish *criteria.*
3 minutes—*Prioritize* criteria.
1 minute—Identify the *options.*
2½ minutes—*Evaluate* the options.
1 minute—*Troubleshoot.*
Total: *10 minutes!*

Hopefully, you will find that by going through this "tight time pressure" analysis, not only is it quick and possibly fun, but you may have come up with an option or, indeed, a "Winner" that you did not think of beforehand. So much for this being a long and cumbersome process!

In using the building blocks under time pressure, follow these important guidelines:

- *Ride the crest of the waves.* When you must make complex decisions in only a few minutes, you may not have time to do any "underwater" exploration. So focus on the outstanding *Achieves, Preserves,* and *Avoids;* assess them for any Absolute Requirements (and make certain these are realistically measurable).
- Try to think of more options than immediately come to mind and evaluate each against the Absolutes, eliminating any option the very first time it fails to meet a Requirement (unless you begin having second doubts about its truly being an Absolute Requirement).
- Be sure to allocate *at least* 60 seconds for Troubleshooting

whatever looks like the best choice(s). This final 1 minute of Troubleshooting can make the difference between success and failure.

- Avoid snap judgments. Question your instincts for reflex action. Take whatever time you have and think through to your solutions *systematically.* The up-front investment of time may more than pay off for you—and certainly programming your mind this way will make performing each analysis second nature to you.

By using these seven Building Blocks under pressure, you can keep your head while others are losing theirs.

THE EMOTIONAL FACTOR: SOLVING PERSONAL PROBLEMS

In resolving highly personal problems, there are certain guidelines that should be followed.

1. Always make sure that your values and ratings represent your true thinking and feeling.
2. If you have doubts after you've arrived at a solution—and time permits—put aside your analysis for a while.
3. Try to find a "sounding board" who can help you sort out your feelings and criteria. It's easier to clarify your values by talking things over with someone who will challenge your feelings and assumptions than by working alone.
4. If at all possible, work through the problem with the people who will be affected. Shared solutions are preferable to solo solutions; it helps ensure commitment and makes effective execution more predictable.
5. Make sure you've considered all the options, even ones that—at least initially—appear improbable.
6. Troubleshoot your decision, including thinking through

how best to make your announcement (to whom, in what setting, in what words, in what time frame, etc.). Foresight should eliminate need for remedial action in hindsight.

GROUP THINK: MAKING DECISIONS EN MASSE

Conclusions should be based on the best available information and not on personal domination of the discussion. In fact, the use of the seven-step Option Analysis Process minimizes the possibility of confrontation, arguments, criticisms, and deceptiveness. The shy, reserved, or fearful person can enter the process at any point, feeling safer and more secure if the seven-step process has been made explicit, visible, and legitimized by whoever is conducting the discussion. It is also because *information* is (or certainly should be) the focus and basis of judgment, not the ability of a participant to "speak the loudest" or "carry the biggest stick."

One of the secrets to the success of Option Analysis is the separation of information from judgment. The seven steps enable you to constantly break everything you are doing in the analysis into two segments: *Describe;* only then *Evaluate.* Ask the process questions, get agreement on the data, *then* discuss and evaluate it.

Don't try to do everything at the same time or you risk applying incorrect or partial data, cutting off and antagonizing others involved in the same discussion or who might have valuable input, discouraging anxious managers or others from opening their mouths and contributing to what could have been a solid decision and plan, and exercising poor judgment. Then let your use of the process with others demonstrate how "safe" it is for those who have been overly cautious in the past to become involved in decision-making discussions.

But what if the options selected go awry? This can happen, because when people have invested so much of their time, effort, resources, and best thinking into reaching a decision, they often find it difficult to imagine that anything could seriously go wrong. The more experienced you are in decision making, the more likely you may be at times to overlook the significance of Step 7, Troubleshooting, especially if the decision feels "so right" in your gut.

Following are ten additional "Dos" when helping others use the decision-making process in a group setting:

1. Try to understand where people are in the decision process. That is, are they smoking out the issues (Step 1)? What is it they are trying to determine (Step 2)? Are they setting or prioritizing criteria (Steps 3 and 4)? Are they identifying and then evaluating options (Steps 5 and 6) or troubleshooting (Step 7)?

2. Then help them further with that particular step, moving forward or back in the decision process as needed. For instance, if the issues and purpose are clear and if the person says, "But I don't know what to do" (i.e., options), you might ask, "Do you think it might be helpful to first talk about what you are trying to *achieve, preserve,* or *avoid* by any action you take?"

3. Accept their feelings of helplessness, or even hopelessness. It doesn't do any good to say, "You shouldn't feel that way." The fact is, they do, so acknowledge their feelings. Ask, "What's got you puzzled? What question(s) are you trying to answer?" Help them identify at which step they are stuck—and move from there.

4. Keep the focus on *their* answering the decision questions, not you—or else *you'll* own the answer, not they.

5. Get the seven-step questions answered as specifically as possible.

6. Listen carefully. If you are not certain about what they

are saying, ask them to repeat it. Test your understanding by repeating what you believe they said and ask if that is correct. Help them clarify fuzziness, vagueness.

7. Make the decision process *visible*. Write the questions and answers down so those involved with the analysis can see and review what they have said. Use an electronic copy board or an easel and chart paper if working with a group, or a writing tablet if working with an individual.

8. Be patient while trying to undersand how they feel and encourage them. Tell them when they are doing well with the process. Reinforce successes, giving nods and other expressions of approval.

9. Treat the feelings they share with you as confidential and assure them of confidentiality. Follow through accordingly.

10. Occasionally test their understanding of what you are doing and *why* you are doing it to be sure they see you as helping and not confusing them. Explain if they are confused.

And now some "Don'ts" to be aware of:

1. Don't be too brisk and businesslike. This process permits such incisiveness that you can come across this way and be threatening to people if you are not careful.

2. Don't set unrealistic expectations.

3. Don't push your own favorite options, taking away the person's right to do this for himself or herself.

4. Don't assume that what you are doing is so logical that everyone will automatically understand and accept it as the only right way to make a decision.

5. Don't allow yourself to be trapped into telling people what you think they should do. When offering criteria, options, and so forth, offer them as suggestions to be evaluated by the person.

6. Don't try to push anyone beyond his or her capacity to absorb and respond effectively to the questions and the process. Because the process works, it is easy to become a zealot in using it, and to overlook the fatigue that other people may feel in a particularly complex analysis. Plan for breaks and set milestones for assessing progress. Process checks can help in detecting where time is not being spent wisely and where things can be speeded up (i.e., where you are versus where you should be in terms of the seven steps).

It often helps to tentatively assign a timekeeper, and then take stock of the productivity of your discussion as you reach each point. You can then compare the amount of time spent with the amount of time you had allotted for completing the particular steps, and judge how to invest your remaining time accordingly.

7. Select where information has been made visible, and a pause in the analysis can be taken before resuming an evaluation. The more specific the information, the easier it should be to pick up just where you left off with no lost motion.

Now let's turn our attention to the third part of the Complete Thought Process—Risk Analysis.

RISK ANALYSIS PROCESS QUESTIONS

1. Which should be evaluated first, impact or probability? Why?
2. Can you take "preventive actions" against "potential risks"?
3. Does "protective action" reduce the probabilities of risk?
4. From where should you derive "Likely Causes"?

Answers to Risk Analysis Questions

1. *Which should be evaluated first, impact or probability? Why?*
   When evaluating the potential risks in terms of impact or probability, you must first evaluate the potential risk in terms of its potential impact. If you only have limited time and budget, then you will want to know which potential risks have the highest impact (severity). Then go on to evaluate the probability of those "High" or "Medium" impacts where time is of the essence. The consequence of a "high impact, medium probability risk" may well be more important to you than the consequence of a "high probability but only medium impact risk."

2. *Can you take "preventive actions" against "potential risks"?*
   You cannot take preventive actions against potential risks, but only against their "likely causes" (i.e., you cannot prevent a fire—only those things that might *cause* a fire).
   On the other hand, protective actions are taken against potential risks. Protective actions typically are set up to be triggered if and when your preventive action has failed to prevent one or more likely causes from occuring and creating the problem, or the problem has been caused by something unanticipated. Thus, to minimize the seriousness of the potential risk, you may wish to set up a protective action.

3. *Does "protective action" reduce the probabilities of risk?*
   Protective action itself does *not* reduce the probability of a risk. It only may reduce the impact of a potential risk should it occur. Some actions, however, are both preventive and protective. The U.S. military stationed in Saudi Arabia in 1990–1991 was both preventive against a

number of likely causes of Saddam Hussein's invading that country and protective in case he did.

4. *From where should you derive "Likely Causes"?*
"Likely Causes" come from your priority potential risks. If a risk is not "high priority," there really is no reason to spend your time looking for the Likely Causes of something that either would not be particularly serious if it did indeed occur or probably is not going to happen.

The importance of Risk Analysis cannot be overstated. If you can effectively troubleshoot a variety of business, home, and personal challenges, think how much more successful you will become! Think of the potential benefit in habitually asking yourself and others, "OK, now what could go wrong?" and then taking preventive action against each Likely Cause that might create one or more possible roadblocks in any of these common situations:

1. Meeting a critical commitment, timetable, or milestone.
2. Presenting a proposal to your boss, a customer, or the board of directors.
3. Making a major change ("major" as defined not necessarily by you but as it might be viewed by the affected people) and then communicating it to employees, family members, or other influential constituencies.
4. Hiring a new manager or a contractor.
5. Meeting someone for a key appointment.
6. Taking a new job.
7. Buying a new piece of equipment (for your company or family).
8. Investing in a stock, company, play, and so forth.
9. Having to postpone or cancel a contract.
10. Making an acquisition or setting up a joint venture.

Following is the Risk Analysis process broken down to its basic questions. Study them, then take a crucial event or decision you face and carry out a Risk Analysis of it. Put yourself under time pressure. Make the questions work for you!

RISK ANALYSIS REVIEW

1. *Scan for and specify potential risks*
   - What are all the potential risks or problems associated with the decision or plan?
   - What are all the opportunities possible?

2. *Prioritize each potential risk or opportunity*
   - What is the severity or impact of each potential risk (or payoff if the opportunity were to present itself)? [High, Medium, or Low?]
   - What is the chance or likelihood of occurrence of each potential risk (or opportunity)? [High, Medium, or Low?]
   - Which are too risky—or represent such an opportunity—and thus are high priority?

3. *Identify the several Likely Causes of each priority potential risk (or opportunity)*
   - What are the Likely Causes of each potential risk (or opportunity)?
   - If there are a lot of Likely Causes, what is the Probability that each of these Likely Causes will occur?
   - Are there lower-level causes that need to be specified for each Probable Cause?

4. *Specify preventive or opportunistic action against each Likely Cause*
   - Will each preventive action really reduce the likelihood that the particular Likely Cause will happen?
   - Will each opportunistic action really raise the likelihood that the Cause will happen?

- Will the actions taken against the Likely Cause really combine to reduce the probability that the risk will happen, or raise the probability that the opportunity will occur?

5. *Specify protective action against high-potential risks, and actions to capitalize on potential opportunities that may occur*
   - Will the protective action minimize the seriousness of the potential risk if it happens?
   - Is there more than one protective action you should set up to be taken against the priority potential risks?
   - What actions can you be ready to implement if certain hoped-for opportunities materialize in order to exploit them?

6. *Refine your plan*
   - What's the best way to implement these actions?
   - Can you integrate these actions with the remainder of the Communication and Implementation Plan to ensure that your decision achieves its criteria?

Troubleshooting forces you to "think the unthinkable." Not only is "forewarned is forearmed," but to the extent that these thoughts prompt you to take actions to ward off dangers, they allow you to implement your decisions with a heightened sense of assurance that you will indeed accomplish your purpose.

What are some of the forthcoming issues, decisions, or events facing you right now—in business or in an organization to which you belong, or with your family or friends—that it would be helpful to troubleshoot? Take 10 minutes and do a "tight time pressure" Risk Analysis in the following format:

1 minute—Scan for potential *risks.*
1 minute—*Prioritize* (impact/likelihood).
3½ minutes—Identify the several *Likely Causes* of each "high impact" and "medium to high" likelihood risk.

2½ minutes—Specify *preventive* or opportunistic actions (to take against each *priority* Likely Cause).

1 minute—Specify *protective* or opportunistic actions (to take against each high-priority potential risk).

1 minute—Refine your plan accordingly.

Total: *10 minutes!*

Were you surprised that the most time—three and a half minutes—should be allocated to "smoking out" likely causes of high-priority risks and opportunities? This likely cause step is at the heart of Risk Analysis. The more specifically you can identify high-likelihood causes, the greater the chance your experience, know-how, and judgment can help you quickly identify feasible ways to prevent them from happening (or the more you can help make opportunities come about). You'll also feel more confident of your ability both in using the process and in managing this situation. Keep using the analyses for all important situations and you should become more and more a winner in every facet of your personal and business life.

EPILOGUE

The Right Choice

In the days before telephones and television, mass transportation, and other elements of modern life, it was easier to make the right choice; after all, there were simply fewer options. The pace of change, however, has accelerated during the past decade in so many respects. And accelerated change has been accompanied by an increasingly wider range of options available to decision makers. That makes it all the more important to have at your disposal an explicit, time-proven decision process.

But we are creatures of habit, which has a positive and a negative side. If we weren't, we would have a most difficult time of surviving every day. After all, if we had to consciously think through every single issue or choice we face, we'd never get anything done! But life has taught us how to make a myriad of decisions with very little thought, from the ritual we follow in arising in the morning and going to work, to greeting friends and business associates, to answering the telephone, to writing a letter, and to conducting a meeting. This is not to say that there aren't thoughtful decisions that have to be made in these activities; but by and large, not a great deal of time needs to be invested in making choices that work.

At the same time, our largely unconscious and habitual ways of thinking through choices predisposes us to making decisions that in the longer run may not be in our best interest. Although they help us cope with life on a day-to-day operating basis, they also tend to keep us in ruts, so we fail to recognize and seize upon innovative alternatives to the historical choices we make, day in and day out.

As individuals, as organizations, and as a nation, we tend to get locked into certain modes of response to situations. But to excel, to strengthen our effectiveness as individuals and organizations, and ultimately to compete more effectively as a nation, we must adopt a more-innovative, yet practical, decision-making process.

Today, there is much talk about why America has become a second-rate country in terms of the global marketplace. The discussion usually focuses on issues such as trade balances, manufacturing techniques, employee empowerment, and other technical issues. In fact, the decision-making process has long been ignored. If we have no explicit means of making key decisions, how can we expect to make the right choices? We can't, which is why companies make foolish acquisitions that simply destroy otherwise viable businesses and spit out people as if they were expendable human "resources."

The lack of an explicit and proven decision system is also the reason that companies spend tens of millions of dollars on products that never had a chance of succeeding, that companies make products with impossibly high design costs or design flaws, and that companies fail to take advantage of their most important asset, their people. Application of the *Complete Thought Process* tools would quickly reveal the folly of so many mistakes that are only appreciated after the fact when it is too late, when companies have been crippled and careers ruined.

The lack of a decision-making process also tends to lead American business leaders to think in terms of the short term. If they were to thoroughly think through their options and risks, they would surely reconsider their decisions regarding R&D, investments, and key strategic planning. Just look at the disastrous state of the banking industry today, and how its eagerness to indulge in risky but expedient and supposedly profitable loans and real estate speculation has become a national disaster.

In addition to serving as a means of making the right internal choices, a systematic decision-making process like the *Complete Thought Process* will be essential in the coming years. Joint ventures and sourcing (i.e., delivering product or components) to geographically distant areas will become increasingly important, and more products will be built by companies working together in many different physical locations, often in different countries and cultural contexts. A common decision-making process can wire participating companies together, integrating and melding culturally distinct groups. Once familiar with the *Complete Thought* steps, networked people may enter the decision process at any point, quickly review progress to date, and contribute to the final choice.

As this book hopefully has demonstrated, the *Complete Thought Process* tools allow you to communicate and make decisions far more effectively—whether alone, in a group, or geographically separated. The tools give you a clear and systematic method for getting to the Root Cause of problems, a method for analyzing your options, and a technique for ensuring that your decisions achieve the desired results. There is *no* conceivable problem or opportunity beyond the scope of the *Complete Thought Process* tools. Using the tools in and of themselves does not guarantee proper judgment or decisions. But applying them should indeed raise the probability of making the right choice, getting buy-in, and taking correct actions.

Of course, many situations in life do not require all of the steps of all three tools. If you've started applying the techniques, it should quickly become second nature to determine which tool to use, when to use it, and how much of it to use. The tools can become integrated into your life in a way that helps mesh your own experience and beliefs, management style, and objectives.

Armed with these tools, you and your colleagues can accomplish anything that you set your minds to. You can make the system work for you, bringing it to bear on any problem you want to resolve with the full benefit of your own and your associates' experience, knowledge, insight, and values. Or you can ignore these techniques and solve problems, make decisions, plan, and communicate the way you always have.

It is my sincere hope that you will choose what's best for you and your future. I encourage you to share your knowledge of and experience with these processes to anybody who could benefit from them. In this way, you can achieve a synergistic or "multiplier" effect for your organization.

If enough companies and government agencies begin applying a systematic decision process to the problems at hand, we will see tremendous strides that result in more-competitive companies, more-satisfying organizational and home life, and a stronger nation participating more effectively in a highly competitive global economy.

The choice is ours.

INDEX